POWER HOUSE

POWER HOUSE

*Strategies for Female Realtors
to Outperform the Industry*

Marcia Bergen

BURMAN BOOKS
MEDIA CORP.

BURMAN BOOKS

MEDIA CORP.

Published 2024 by Gildan Media LLC, aka G&D Media
by arrangement with Burman Books Media Corp.
www.GandDmedia.com

Edited by Lara Petersen
Cover Photos by Melanie Vanheyst
Book Design by Clarissa D'Costa

Library of Congress Cataloging-in-Publication Data is available upon request

ISBN: 978-1-7225-9904-1

10 9 8 7 6 5 4 3 2 1

CONTENTS

CHAPTER ONE
The Tools in the Toolbox

"Progress lies not in enhancing what is,
but in advancing toward what will be."
—Khalil Gibran

In the realm of entrepreneurship, the journey toward building your own business is akin to constructing a sturdy edifice, brick by brick. The practice of real estate takes careful planning and meticulous execution to build from the ground up, just as your entrepreneurial endeavors require thoughtful consideration and deliberate action.

I reminisce upon pivotal moments of my own journey, and one instance lingers vividly in my mind: the day I opened an email to discover that I had attained the esteemed position of being among the top one percent in sales amidst the other 2,400 agents within my sales district. The gravity of this achievement weighed heavily upon me, causing my mouth to parch instantly, my eyes to well up with tears, and my knees to weaken. Time seemed to stand still, and a profound silence enveloped the room. In that moment, I yearned to encapsulate its essence and forever carry it within the depths of my pockets. This achievement signified the culmination of my aspirations and embodied all the hopes and dreams I had harbored since the early days of my real estate career. It was a definitive milestone—a bookmark in time; however, this journey of mine, like any other, was not devoid of trials and tribulations. There were victories to celebrate, defeats to endure, lessons to learn, and sacrifices to make. My journey was a rollercoaster ride that demanded resilience and unwavering determination.

Before delving into the reasons you are contemplating a new business venture in real estate sales or reinvigorating your existing one—a venture that is intricately guided, molded, and shaped by your vision—it is paramount to provide some insight into my personal background. By doing so, I will foster an understanding that I am no different than you, and you are no different than me. We share common aspirations and dreams. I stand neither above nor below you. Each path you follow in pursuit of your personal destination is one I have already traveled. Though our journeys may diverge, and you may encounter smoother roads than I did, we are united by the emotions, passions, and goals that drive us toward success.

I am often approached with inquiries about my humble beginnings in the realm of real estate and how I managed to swiftly construct my business. As I reflect upon those early days, the truth is that I was burdened by my fear of failure and the constant pressure I put on myself to succeed. The burden was so heavy that my recollection of the meticulous planning and mental processes that propelled me forward in the first two years is rather hazy. To be completely honest, during that time, I was torn between dedicating myself fully to the business and contemplating a return to my nine-to-five corporate real estate job.

This internal struggle persisted for a good three years. I often wonder how much faster my business would have grown if I had only possessed the ability and willingness to immerse myself entirely in the mindset of a commission-based salesperson. The nagging uncertainty after every sale—"Will anyone ever reach out to me again to buy or sell a house?"—was a palpable reality and remained my reality until I wholeheartedly embraced the mindset that allowed me to construct the systems necessary for consistent results. These are the very systems I am eager to share with you.

Allow me to share some of my background to serve as a reference as you navigate the chapters ahead. Use it as a compass to reaffirm that we all embark on our journeys from similar starting points and are driven by comparable aspirations.

First, there is no judgment here. My beliefs belong to me, just as yours belong to you. Second, consider this manual a tool to expedite your journey toward achieving your goals, minimizing distractions and heartaches, fostering respect, and ultimately leading to success.

I spent my formative years in a small town in southeastern Manitoba, nestled near the heart of Canada. Born into a Mennonite lineage, my roots were firmly grounded in modesty. My grandparents toiled as farmers, and eventually, my mother's family farm transformed into a residential subdivision within a suburban hamlet.

Two years after I was born, my parents welcomed a second child, which bestowed upon me the role of an elder sister and the leader of our little tribe. Unfortunately, my father, plagued by alcoholism, left my mother battered and our family deprived of basic necessities such as food and safety. I was three years old when my mother summoned the courage to save herself, me, and my little brother from a life marred by harrowing abuse. She divorced my father, who tragically passed away a few years later when I was eleven. My connection with him was nonexistent, but the memories I carry comprise the traumatic residue etched within me—speeding cars that trigger anxiety, the scent of whiskey on someone's breath, and the overwhelming sensations of fear and solitude.

When I was five years old, my mother remarried and I was instantly a member of a blended family. After transitioning from the eldest child to a middle child, I mastered the art of negotiation, a skill acquired through navigating the intricacies of a stepsibling dynamic, particularly with an older stepsister and stepbrother by my side.

I was always an incorrigible dreamer—headstrong and adorned with a sharp mind and a plethora of opinions. During my teenage years, my sights were set on a career in journalism and aspirations of eventually pursuing law. To that end, I secured my first job and resolved to save for the day when I would graduate and embark on this path. This choice deviated from the trajectory my parents had taken. While both achieved success in their respective pursuits, neither pursued higher education—my stepfather, in fact, never even graduated from high school. Together, my mother and stepfather toiled tirelessly, building a business in commercial finishing, while my mother maintained a job as a secretary in the very elementary and middle school I attended. Perhaps, due to their limited opportunities to pursue their goals and ultimate dreams, they were not particularly encouraging when it came to supporting my idea of getting a university education.

Growing up, I felt compelled to suppress many of my opinions, and there was little room in our household for discussions on races or religions outside the confines of our immediate families. For someone bursting with ideas, goals, and dreams, this proved to be incredibly painful.

At the age of fifteen, my life took an unexpected turn when I got pregnant. I got married just two weeks after my 16th birthday, and by autumn I was a mother. I distinctly recall that, soon after I disclosed my pregnancy, my parents arranged a meeting with my now ex-husband and his parents. Due to their religious beliefs, they saw no alternative but for me to marry, and thus voluntarily relinquished their parental rights. As one can imagine, a marriage between a sixteen-year-old and a nineteen-year-old was far from ideal.

With the assistance of my in-laws, my new husband and I became homeowners and bearers of a mortgage overnight. We worked relentlessly to personalize our home and transform it into a space we could be proud to raise our son in. Over the next four years, I endured emotional and physical abuse. I was subjected to relentless insults. I was labeled as stupid, fat, and ugly. My world grew increasingly restricted until my sole focus revolved around caring for our son, working a part-time job, and tending to the household and yard. There was little room for me to further my education.

Looking back, I can confidently say that this was the loneliest period of my life. I confided in my parents and shared the hardships I endured, only to be met with their refusal to intervene or offer assistance in extricating myself from the situation I had unwittingly fallen into—a situation I had no way of knowing or comprehending what true sacrifices and costs it would demand. After four years, and after giving birth to a daughter, I discovered that my husband was expecting a child with another woman.

I cannot precisely pinpoint the moment when the realization struck that this life was not meant to be mine. I had long relinquished the notion of practicing law or pursuing any form of higher education. Leaving high school to marry meant that my highest academic achievement was a General Education Development certificate, which I pursued a couple of years into my marriage. My dreams had been crushed, but the essence of my soul persisted—the stubborn, opinionated teenager I was before the bad situation unfolded.

About three months after I learned that my husband was having an affair, a moment presented itself—a cosmic calling beckoned me toward my true life's purpose and direction. As you embark on the journey of self-invention, you will encounter several similar moments—instances when your soul implores your mind to align with it. These are the times when your spirit, like a lobster, outgrows its shell. You will shed what no longer serves you to redefine your values and yourself.

I spent over four arduous years immersed in the intricacies of finalizing my divorce. This period proved to be an invaluable teacher, revealing profound lessons that would shape my future. It became evident that people's professed love and support were often contingent upon how well it aligned with their own agendas. When their self-interests were threatened, they swiftly discarded me and prioritized the preservation of their own values and beliefs. Although, unbeknownst to me at the time, this lesson would prove instrumental in my future business endeavors by honing my ability to connect and disconnect with individuals.

At the tender age of twenty-one, I felt as though I had lived a lifetime, learning more profound lessons than many individuals I encountered who were older, ostensibly wiser, and had greater life experiences under their belts. I was blessed with two beautiful children, and yet I found myself without a practical means of providing for them coupled with minimal support from my family. For a few months, my parents let me live with them as I diligently sought employment, arranged childcare, secured a place to live, and fought tooth and nail to get a fair share of marital assets to furnish my new apartment.

By the time I turned twenty-four, with my mother's support, I enrolled in college and started a paralegal program. While it fell short of a law degree, it aligned with the field I had always yearned to be a part of. The program bridged the void that existed within the shattered remnants of my past hopes and dreams that had been sacrificed at the altar of marriage and motherhood.

Following the completion of an intensive ten-month program at a local career college, I swiftly secured a position with a lawyer who was transitioning from property development to establishing a new practice in our shared hometown. Little did I know that this job and this man would provide my first taste of genuine support and mentorship, breaking the mold of my prior experiences. Under the guidance of Mr. H, I spent a total of six years immersing myself in the nuances of real estate law, delving into accounting to manage the firm's financials, and nurturing the growth of the practice alongside him. As life unfolded, personal challenges emerged and cast shadows over my career trajectory with him. Upon reflection, this turning point proved to be both a blessing and a curse wrapped in a single package. Those challenges forced me to expand my horizons and embark on a journey that ultimately led me to where I stand today, while simultaneously causing me to relinquish the safety net of familiarity and comfort that I had grown accustomed to.

As I embarked on a new chapter in Winnipeg, a mere 45-minute journey from my previous residence, my son had entered the realm of adolescence while my daughter stood on the precipice of her teenage years. At this juncture, I welcomed my second son into the world in hopes of salvaging a failing relationship. Alas, that endeavor also crumbled, which left me in my early thirties and single yet again. This time I found myself navigating the intricacies of shared custody for my two eldest children, under less-than-ideal circumstances, while simultaneously striving to establish an amicable co-parenting dynamic with the father of my third child.

For a brief stint, I toiled at a mid-sized law firm before transitioning into the role of a paralegal and office manager. I was entrusted with overseeing a vast retail real estate portfolio that belonged to a family in one of the eastern provinces. Single-handedly shouldering the weight of the firm's responsibilities, I operated as a one-woman army managing the day-to-day operations. This arrangement gave me the flexibility to accommodate my children's appointments and school schedules, all while maintaining a career that granted us a modest yet comfortable existence. We enjoyed the stability of home-ownership, a reliable vehicle, well-stocked fridges, cherished family vacations, and uninterrupted access to utilities.

Over the ensuing years, I stumbled through a series of relationships, igniting and extinguishing the flames of matrimony. It is with a tinge of embarrassment that I admit my inability to provide my children with the stability of consistent father figures or reliable mentors. The scars of abuse and the weight of ill-fated relationship choices had eroded my self-esteem and rendered me incapable of making sound decisions when it came to inviting men into my life.

In 2003, I attained my real estate license, thus commencing a decade-long tenure predominantly catering to property

developers and national property managers, and adeptly negotiating leases on behalf of landlords while diligently tending
to the manifold expectations of tenants and property owners.
Then, in 2011, I made a pivotal shift into residential sales.
As you will discover in the forthcoming chapters, I was ill-
prepared but filled with good intentions. My personal circumstances presented their own set of challenges: a son grappling
with drug addiction, a daughter navigating the complexities of
teenage self-discovery, and a high-strung young son attending
primary school. I was a single parent with a mortgage, limited
credit, and a scarce understanding of the sacrifices that lay
ahead.

Late nights and early mornings became the norm as I
strived to balance my responsibilities as a mother while diligently building my career. Along this arduous journey, I
acquired invaluable knowledge and forged connections with
remarkable individuals who would later become extended
family, friends, and unwavering supporters in my future business endeavors.

By 2014, I had risen to the ranks of the top three percent of agents in my industry, and by 2016, I ascended to the
coveted top one percent. To put this achievement into perspective, it is worth noting that during this time, there were
approximately 1,800 real estate agents operating within my
region.

In the process of penning this book, my utmost desire
has been for you to find resonance with your own authentic
truths and values. Within these pages, I will help you discover
the essential framework necessary to construct not only your
business but also your personal brand. It is my sincerest aspi-
ration that this narrative grants you a realistic self-perception
and ignites a burning ambition to forge a life and career that
fills you with profound pride. Now that you have reached this
point, I want you to know that I am your unwavering cheerleader. I am here on the sidelines, filled with confidence that
you will arrive precisely at the destination you desire and

deserve—a place defined solely by your own unwavering principles and truths.

I am intimately acquainted with the trials and tribulations that life can throw your way, and I understand the vital
importance of a support system that uplifts and sustains you.
As you embark on this journey, I cannot contain my excitement for the moment when you emerge on the other side,
having authored your own story—the story of your remarkable impact as a leader and a beacon of inspiration for women
everywhere. Your boundless capabilities to effect change
in both your personal and professional spheres fill me with
anticipation. Know that I am you, just as you are me, and
together we exemplify the guiding light for every woman seeking to script or redefine her own narrative.

Let's journey together.

CHAPTER ONE
The Tools in the Toolbox

*"Progress lies not in enhancing what is,
but in advancing toward what will be."*
—Khalil Gibran

CHAPTER SUMMARY
This chapter introduced you to my origin story and journey through challenges, relationships, and transitions that ultimately led to a successful career in real estate. Drawing from a powerful quote from Khalil Gibran about progress, I compared entrepreneurship to the construction of a building. This journey is filled with adversity, heartbreak, victories, and learning moments, all which demand resilience and determination. I discussed the personal struggles I had to overcome on my path toward success. This chapter set the stage for the lessons and stories to come, and the wisdom derived from these personal and professional experiences. This intimate look at my early life included hardship, abuse, early motherhood, divorce, and eventually, success in real estate.

REFLECTION QUESTIONS
1. Did any aspect of this chapter resonate with your own experiences? How?
2. What is your concept of success?
3. How do you think my approach to entrepreneurship was shaped by my personal experiences? In what ways does this relate to your own story?

EMPOWERING YOUR ENTREPRENEURIAL JOURNEY: THE FEAR-TRAP QUIZ

In the early days of my real estate journey, I was burdened by immense personal pressure and the fear of failure. This exercise is intended for you to explore some common fears that entrepreneurs face when they start out. I encourage you to complete these sentences with full, raw honesty.

1. My biggest fear about starting my own business is:
2. The most exciting aspect of being an entrepreneur is:
3. The primary task I foresee occupying most of my time as an entrepreneur is:
4. As I immerse myself in entrepreneurship, I am:
5. I feel anxious about being:
6. I worry that if my business fails:
7. If my entrepreneurial venture succeeds, my family will:
8. If I admit my frustrations, I am upset that I:
9. One reason I feel apprehensive about this journey is:

Reflect on these responses. As you do, consider for whom you are embarking on this difficult but rewarding journey. Where is the fear really coming from?

TO-DO LIST

- Reflect on your responses to the fear-trap quiz and write down any parallels to the experiences listed in Chapter One.
- Identify key learning points from this exercise that could inform your entrepreneurship journey.
- Identify any personal or professional obstacles in your path and brainstorm strategies to overcome them.
- Research more about the real estate industry in your region, or your chosen industry, and consider the tools you will need to equip yourself with to be successful.

- Think about the goals you would like to achieve in this course and in your personal and professional life. Jot these goals down. You will formalize and review these as you work through the chapters.

STEP-BY-STEP INSTRUCTIONS

1. Read Chapter One and take note of things that stand out to you.
2. Complete the exercises and take time to reflect.
3. Work through the to-do list and set actionable goals to complete each task.
4. Reflect on your goals as you go through this process to ensure that your business strategy aligns with those goals.

TIPS AND TAKEAWAYS

- Treat challenges as opportunities for learning and growth.
- Everyone's journey to success is unique and filled with ups and downs.
- Resilience is a key trait in successful entrepreneurship.
- Stay focused on your goals, but be willing to adjust your path as needed.
- Seek mentorship and guidance from those who have traveled a similar path.

Your own tips and takeaways:

- _____
  _____
- _____
  _____
- _____
  _____

CHAPTER TWO
Wrestling the Myth Beast

"Illusions commend themselves to us because they save us pain and allow us to enjoy pleasure instead. We must therefore accept it without complaint when they sometimes collide with a bit of reality against which they are dashed to pieces."
—**Sigmund Freud**

UNVEILING THE REALITIES OF OWNING A COMMISSION-BASED REAL ESTATE BUSINESS

Industry experts have conducted research that sheds light on the challenging nature of the residential real estate commission side of business. According to their estimates, approximately 90 percent of realtors quit working in the industry within their first few years. This daunting statistic highlights the fierce competition and demanding nature of the industry. On the flip side, the other 10 percent of real estate agents manage to secure 90 percent of the business, showcasing the concentrated success within the industry.

As I ventured into the world of residential real estate, I embarked on a journey full of uncertainties. I had no defined goals, no structured business plan, and no clients to rely on. Armed with a small sovereign's check from my previous employer, along with my experience in business management and negotiation skills, I decided to take the plunge. The first step was to affiliate myself with a registered broker to ensure that my existing real estate license remained active. I was aware that if my license lapsed for more than a year, I would be required to start the training course from scratch—an unproductive and costly setback.

While this was going on, I was also in the process of selling a sizable family home in a central neighborhood. My intention was to downsize to a more suitable accommodation for myself and my two youngest children. Little did I know that my "stable" job would vanish overnight when I was unexpectedly escorted out of the premises, clutching my final paycheck. I was suddenly unemployed, caught off guard by the swift turn of events.

As I contemplated my options, I toyed with the idea of taking a year off to recalibrate and determine the next step in my career. This would mean relying on unemployment insurance and navigating life within a tight budget. After climbing the corporate ladder in the real estate world, capitalizing on my paralegal, accounting, and management background, I had grown comfortable in my position, but it had been out of financial necessity rather than a genuine passion for the job that propelled my ascension. And just like that, my comfort zone shattered.

With a meager $11,000 in my bank account, I knew I could stretch that amount to cover my expenses for only three or four months. Drawing upon my experience of scraping by and sustaining my family with an income barely sufficient to cover rent and put food on the table for two young children, I resolved to make this work. I harnessed my resourcefulness and honed skills like repurposing discarded furniture into usable pieces and transforming paper grocery bags into vintage bows to adorn the family Christmas tree. My ability to cook and bake from scratch proved invaluable in stretching every dollar. The struggles of the past had equipped me with a resilient mindset—I was ready to face this challenge head-on.

Reflecting upon my circumstances, I questioned whether I had been ill-informed about the financial implications of starting a commission-based business with such limited funds, or if I had simply been naïve. At the time, I had a mortgage to consider, a car payment to make, and two dependent children. Looking back, I wish I had possessed the courage to face the woman I was back then. She possessed a reservoir of courage and strength that I now truly comprehend.

MYTH #1

The first myth that needs to be shattered when venturing into any new business is the expectation of consistent and immediate cash flow. This is especially true in the real estate industry. In fact, not only will money fail to flow in consistently, but each month you will incur broker and association fees.

Allow me to paint a picture of what a $10,000 commission check looks like. Opting for a 75/25 split with your broker means that you can avoid or minimize costs related to signage, Multiple Listing Service (MLS) fees, and monthly desk fees; however, when you finally receive payment, that $10,000 shrinks to $7,500.

A significant portion of new agents choose the 75/25 split to mitigate the burden of monthly costs, which can accumulate rapidly during the initial months of business when sales may be scarce. These costs can easily deplete any excess revenue that trickles into your account.

On the other hand, a 95/5 split with your broker requires you to shoulder all expenses related to signage, MLS fees, advertising, and desk fees. Desk fees can range from $500 to $1,800 per month, depending on the services offered by your brokerage. In this scenario, receiving a $10,000 payment translates to approximately $9,500 after deducting administration fees, which generally amount to 1–2 percent of the commission.

Before deciding where to place your license, interview multiple brokers and gain a comprehensive understanding of the costs associated with each. Some brokerages offer exceptional coaching and in-house training, while others follow a low-cost, minimal-service model. Exploring different options will help you align your short-term goals and values with the brokerage that best suits your needs. It is not uncommon for agents to switch brokerages once they have acquired some experience and a clearer vision of their business trajectory.

Another avenue worth considering is joining a real estate team. These teams often provide opportunities for placement at little or no cost, along with lead-generation support. This option proves beneficial in two ways: you can avoid incurring expenses during the first year or two of your career, unlike solo agents, and you gain access to training and shadowing opportunities that expedite the learning process that enables you to engage in transactions sooner. However, if personal exposure and seeing your name on a property sign are pivotal to your aspirations, joining a team may not align with your ego-driven goals.

Choosing a career in real estate demands an understanding of the mythological beast that awaits. Wrestling with the realities of the industry involves acknowledging the scarce and unpredictable cash flow, along with the ongoing financial obligations. By embracing the truth and adopting a strategic approach, aspiring real estate agents can navigate the path to success.

Beyond the brokerage fees, aspiring agents should be aware of the various expenses they will incur on their entrepreneurial journey. While this list is not exhaustive, it includes some of the significant costs associated with the profession:

MARKETING

As a new agent, invest in marketing to establish your brand and generate leads. While the specific avenues for marketing can vary based on your target market, here are some general avenues you can explore, along with associated costs:

Website: Create a professional website to bolster your online presence. Costs vary depending on whether you build it yourself using website builders (e.g., Wix, WordPress) or hire a web developer/designer. Costs range from a few hundred to several thousand dollars.

Business Cards and Printed Materials: Designing and printing business cards, brochures, flyers, and other promotional materials are traditional marketing methods. Costs depend on the quantity, quality, and design complexity. You can expect to spend a few hundred dollars on printing.

Online Advertising: Digital advertising can be effective in reaching a wider audience. Platforms like Google Ads and social media platforms offer various advertising options, including pay-per-click campaigns. Costs vary based on your target market, geographic location, and ad campaign budget. It is advisable to start small and gradually increase your budget as you see positive results.

Social Media Marketing: Creating and managing social media accounts (e.g., Facebook, Instagram, LinkedIn) is a cost-effective way to connect with potential clients. While it is free to create accounts, you may want to allocate a budget for paid promotions, sponsored posts, or social media management tools to enhance your reach and engagement.

Print and Online Directories: Listing yourself in local real estate directories, both online and in print, can help increase your visibility. Costs depend on the publication or directory you choose, with prices ranging from a few hundred to a few thousand dollars per year.

Networking Events: Attending industry events, conferences, and local networking groups help you build relationships and generate leads. Costs include event registration fees, travel expenses, and promotional materials for the events.

Content Marketing: Creating valuable content, such as blog posts, videos, or podcasts, establish you as an expert and attract potential clients. Costs include content creation tools, video equipment, or outsourcing content creation if needed.

Marketing costs vary significantly depending on your target market, competition, and personal preferences. Set a budget and track your return on investment to ensure you are allocating resources effectively. As you gain experience and refine your marketing strategy, you can optimize your spending to focus on the channels that yield the best results for your real estate business.

Outside of the strategies you will acquire in order to effectively market yourself, you should consider further expenses.

TRANSPORTATION
As a real estate agent, you can expect that increased driving will result in higher vehicle expenses. Here are some key factors to consider when budgeting for vehicle expenses:

Fuel Costs: With increased mileage, you will need to allocate a significant portion of your budget to fuel expenses. Monitor gas prices and estimate your monthly fuel consumption based on your average mileage. You can use online fuel cost calculators or smartphone apps to estimate these costs more accurately.

Maintenance and Repairs: Regular maintenance keeps your vehicle in good condition and avoid breakdowns. Budget for routine services such as oil changes, tire rotations, filter replacements, and brake inspections. Additionally, set aside funds for unexpected repairs that may arise. It is advisable to have an emergency fund for unforeseen vehicle issues.

Insurance: As a real estate agent, you will likely need a comprehensive auto insurance policy that covers both personal and business use. The cost of insurance varies depending on your location, driving record, vehicle type, and coverage limits. Get quotes from multiple insurance providers to compare prices and coverage options.

Vehicle Depreciation: Driving more will accelerate your vehicle's depreciation. Depreciation refers to the decline in value over time. While it is not a direct out-of-pocket expense, when budgeting, consider the impact on your vehicle's resale value.

Parking and Tolls: Depending on your market and the areas you operate in, you may encounter parking fees and tolls. Account for these expenses, especially if you frequently visit urban areas or gated communities where paid parking is prevalent.

Vehicle Upgrades: As your real estate business grows, you might consider upgrading your vehicle to accommodate clients and enhance your professional image. This could include purchasing a larger vehicle, adding signage or wraps, or investing in technology like GPS systems or mobile office setups. Set aside funds for these potential upgrades, taking into account both the initial investment and ongoing maintenance costs.

To manage your vehicle expenses effectively, it is advisable to track your mileage, keep detailed records of maintenance and repairs, and regularly review your budget. By understanding and accounting for these costs, you can ensure that your vehicle remains reliable and that your real estate business remains financially sustainable.

MLS AND LOCAL BOARD FEES

Multiple listing fees and insurance costs are associated with being a real estate agent. Here's an overview of these expenses:

Multiple Listing Service Fees: Many local real estate boards require agents to pay fees for access to the MLS, which is a comprehensive database of properties listed for sale. MLS fees vary depending on the region and the specific board you belong to. These fees are typically paid annually or quarterly and contribute to the operational costs of the MLS system.

Errors and Omissions (E&O) Insurance: E&O insurance is crucial for real estate agents as it provides liability coverage in the event of errors, omissions, or negligence related to your professional services. It protects you and your clients from financial loss that result from legal claims. The cost of E&O insurance will depend on your location, coverage limits, deductible, and personal claims history. It is important to get multiple insurance quotes and select the policy that provides adequate coverage for your specific needs.

General Liability Insurance: In addition to E&O insurance, you should also consider getting general liability insurance. This insurance coverage protects you against third-party claims for property damage or bodily injury that may occur during property showings or other business activities. The cost of general liability insurance varies based on coverage limits, deductible, and your business's size and operations.

Professional Association Membership Fees: Joining professional real estate associations, such as the National Association of Realtors or local real estate boards, often involves membership fees. These fees contribute to the association's services, advocacy efforts, and educational resources. The costs of membership vary depending on the association and its benefits.

Continuing Education Costs: Real estate agents are often required to complete continuing education courses to maintain their licenses. These courses help keep agents updated on industry regulations, market trends, and professional best practices. Continuing education costs can include course fees, study materials, and exam fees. The expenses vary depending on the requirements of your region or licensing authority.

Consider these fees and insurance costs when budgeting for your business. They are essential investments in your professional development, legal protection, and access to valuable resources. Research and compare options to find the most suitable and cost-effective solutions for your specific needs.

Consider the broad scope of financial implications of starting a commission-based business. If you currently have no reserves or immediate access to cash, it may not be the ideal time to enter the real estate industry or any other commission-based profession. Rather than letting this discourage you, use it as motivation to establish a solid financial foundation. Being financially secure will enable you to focus on serving your clients' best interests instead of worrying about mundane expenses like fuel for your vehicle. Take a moment to envision your financial situation six months from now. Consider how you will manage rent or mortgage payments, utilities, and groceries while trying to attract clients and close deals. It is important to note that, even if you are fortunate enough to close a deal on your very first day in the business, you will not receive payment until 30 to 60 days after the possession date. This means that if you have an offer accepted with a 90 day possession date, it could be a lot more than three months before you see that money.

Understanding the timeline for receiving commission checks highlights the importance of having a financial cushion to cover your expenses for at least three to six months. It also underscores the need to be an effective money manager. Consider every dollar saved equivalent to a dollar earned. Review your expenses and identify areas where you can reduce unnecessary spending or negotiate lower debt payments. If feasible, consider getting a roommate to offset rent or mortgage costs. Some agents opt to work part-time jobs during their initial months in real estate, believing it will alleviate financial pressure, but this approach can hinder your overall success. Splitting your focus between two jobs delays your progress in understanding the industry's intricacies, paperwork, and systems. The longer it takes for you to gain momentum and navigate the learning curve, the longer it will take to achieve success. Consider that your time and effort inputted will have a direct correlation to the timeliness of your business growth and, ultimately, your financial stability.

If you are contemplating a second job while pursuing a real estate career, take the time to conduct thorough research. Whether you can pursue another job alongside real estate depends on your location and the specific rules and regulations governing your area. Regulations regarding additional sources of income can vary depending on your location and the specific rules set by your local board. For example, when I began my career in real estate, my local board did not allow realtors to have a second source of income. This rule has since changed to align with the rest of Canada's regulations.

Before embarking on a commission-based real estate business, it is imperative to grasp the financial realities and prepare accordingly. By establishing a solid financial foundation, managing your expenses wisely, and focusing on building your real estate career, you can overcome challenges and position yourself for long-term success.

In my own experience, I was fortunate to list three homes and act for one buyer within the first month of obtaining my real estate license. This initial success provided me with a cushion and leverage. It allowed me to breathe a little easier and focus on securing future business. Despite this early success, I remained diligent in budgeting and maintaining a financial cushion to ensure that I could prioritize my clients' interests without constant financial stress. Through careful management and by taking things month by month and transaction by transaction, I managed to navigate my first year in the business.

MYTH #2

Let's address a second common myth or belief about the real estate industry—that it offers flexibility in terms of setting your own hours. As I write this, I cannot help but chuckle silently in my mind. While it is true that you can block personal time in your calendar, the reality is that you need to remain as flexible as possible to meet your clients' needs. Your clients will include individuals who have jobs, are raising families, and may be caring for elderly parents. They are navigating the complexities of adulthood, and their schedules will dictate the times you meet or show properties. To provide excellent service, you must be flexible and available to your clients whenever possible.

For those agents who believe they can maintain another job while juggling their clients' schedules, the challenge becomes even more formidable. When building your business, your primary goal should be flexibility, availability, and presence for your clients. You will serve as a lifeline for your clients as they make some of their most significant financial decisions. Maintaining another job while trying to meet the needs of your clients creates additional hurdles that can hinder your success.

It is important to note that, aside from showing properties, writing offers, and listing homes, you will also need to focus on building your brand and business plan. While showings and listings are the parts of the business that ultimately lead to payment, a foundational business needs to be constructed and nurtured for these transactional activities to occur and continue. Writing your business plan and working on lead generation spheres are crucial components of the first year of your real estate business and require ongoing attention throughout your career. It is advisable to dedicate four to six hours a day for business-building activities. In future chapters, I will outline these activities in more detail and provide guidance on creating an effective business plan and strategy.

In summary, finding a balance between other commitments and building a successful real estate business requires careful consideration. Understanding the regulations governing additional income sources, recognizing the importance of flexibility for clients, and dedicating sufficient time to business-building activities are key factors in achieving long-term success in the industry.

Embarking on a career in real estate is an exciting venture, and in the first year, you may naturally attract some clients. It is a time of enthusiasm and exploration as you establish yourself in the industry.

As you enter your second year, you will learn much more and experience overall growth. By this point, you should feel more confident in your abilities. You will have a clearer perspective on the systems you built and a larger vision for your business. The second year is where you refine your skills and expand your knowledge base.

Moving into the third year, you will see organic growth and increased volume in your business due to the consistency and effectiveness of the systems you established. Your business will flourish as you build upon your previous experiences and continue managing your operations.

These time frames are not set in stone and are likely to change depending on your natural talents and past experiences in areas like relationship-building, office management, or sales. The reference to years is intended to provide a realistic framework for understanding how your business might progress.

In the realm of real estate, you will wear many hats. Starting this business, or any other business, means taking on various roles. You will be the accountant, the maintenance person, the therapist, the negotiator, and the marketing department, among other things. Flexibility is key as you navigate your clients' needs while simultaneously attending to the tasks required to establish and grow your business.

When I started my real estate business, I had a seven-year-old and a teenager at home. This meant juggling family commitments such as school and extracurricular activities. I had to make sacrifices and often missed social events in order to accommodate my clients. I frequently had to skip my son's hockey games and even wedding dress shopping for my daughter. I became accustomed to arriving late for dinner parties and hesitated to commit to too many events without a prior apology and the possibility of rescheduling.

Networking plays a significant role in letting people know about your real estate business. At times, you will have to make decisions about prioritizing events, such as choosing between a girlfriend's birthday party and a networking event. Such choices need to be planned and scheduled into your calendar to ensure you effectively balance personal and professional obligations.

For me, establishing set office hours from Monday to Friday was a highly effective strategy. This provided me with a dedicated workspace free from distractions and immersed me in the business environment. I utilized this time to plan my daily, weekly, and monthly marketing strategies, write blogs, and create packages to send to lenders and lawyers to generate more business. While these tasks may seem less glamorous than the vision of Selling Sunset or other popular HGTV shows, they greatly contribute to your success. Paying attention to these areas of your business will enable you to grow more quickly and handle a higher volume of clients when you become busy.

Building a real estate business requires commitment, focus, and a balance between personal and professional responsibilities. By embracing the various roles, establishing effective systems, and dedicating time to marketing and business planning, you can navigate the journey of growth and achieve success in the industry.

MYTH #3

A common myth in the real estate industry is the belief that knowing a lot of people automatically translates into having a lot of clients. When your phone isn't ringing off the hook and the people you expected would reach out to you remain silent, you will see how this myth is quickly dispelled.

First and foremost, understand that your family and friends do not owe you their business. This may be a hard pill to swallow, but it is an important reality to accept. Let's consider a scenario: you have a fantastic hair stylist who always gives you the perfect cut and color. Now, imagine your sister becomes a hair stylist. Would you immediately switch stylists? Some people might, while others would choose to stay with their current stylist. This example highlights that personal relationships and trust play significant roles in client decisions, regardless of existing connections.

Over the years and through my experience of building a business, I can assure you that some people who initially hesitated to work with you may change their minds over time. As those around you observe your commitment to the business and witness the time and energy you invest in thoughtful planning and marketing, some of them may decide to work with you. This is where your value proposition becomes your lifeline.

People in your life may already have established relationships with real estate agents they trust. Additionally, some friends and family members are private about their finances and may not feel comfortable discussing their buying or selling intentions with you. Your immediate sphere of influence may not value your opinion as a newly licensed agent unless you provide them with a compelling reason to do so. Building trust and credibility takes time, so stay the course.

A former colleague once told me, "One deal does not a career make." This statement resonates with me deeply. Even though I was a seasoned and successful agent, all my siblings have purchased homes or properties without utilizing my services. One bought a home privately, and the other two used the listing agents for their respective properties. I mention this not out of malice or disappointment but to emphasize that even those closest to you may not choose to work with you.

When building my practice, I focused on providing value and knowledge without plastering a sign on my forehead that said, "Buy and Sell with Me." By adopting a perspective of offering information and advice, I organically built a clientele. Here's an example: I regularly hosted a casual mom's group in my home where we enjoyed wine and conversation. As an avid renovator, I was frequently asked for advice on paint colors, kitchen contractors, and overall renovation guidance. This allowed me to demonstrate my knowledge of increasing a home's value, which in turn showcased my ability to help clients maximize their equity. Notice that I never had to ask, "Are you thinking of selling your home?" or "Do you want to buy a home?" It happened naturally through meaningful interactions.

Engaging in meaningful interactions is a great approach to expanding your network. Volunteering in community organizations, such as your child's school or a local community club, not only allows you to contribute to your community but also provides opportunities to connect with potential clients in a more organic and non-intrusive manner. Building trust and rapport through your volunteer work can lead to valuable referrals and business opportunities.

Creating and participating in informal groups with a shared interest, like professional groups, clothing swap groups, or food drive groups, is also an excellent way to meet new people and expand your network. By engaging in activities that demonstrate your genuine care and concern for the community, you can build meaningful connections with like-minded individuals. Approach these groups with a genuine desire to connect and help others, rather than solely focusing on personal gain.

Here are a few additional suggestions to expand your network:

Attend industry events and conferences. Participating in real estate conferences, trade shows, and networking events provides opportunities to connect with fellow professionals, potential clients, and industry influencers. Be active in conversations, exchange contact information, and follow up with those you meet to cultivate relationships.

Join professional associations. Joining local real estate associations or industry-specific organizations can provide networking opportunities and access to educational resources and professional development. Actively participate in association events, committees, and forums to meet fellow professionals and build connections.

Host community events and seminars. Organize informative seminars and community events related to real estate topics of interest. This positions you as an expert in the field and allows you to connect with potential clients who attend these events. Collaborate with local businesses, community organizations, or schools to maximize reach and impact.

Utilize social media and online platforms. Establish a strong online presence through platforms like LinkedIn, Facebook, Instagram, and Twitter. Share valuable content, engage with your audience, and actively participate in industry-related groups and discussions. This can help you expand your network beyond your immediate circles and reach a wider audience.

Leverage client referrals. Once you have established a client base, ask satisfied clients for referrals. Word-of-mouth recommendations can be powerful in generating new leads and expanding your network. Offer exceptional service and maintain strong relationships to encourage clients to refer you to their friends, family, and colleagues.

Building a network takes time and effort. Focus on providing value, being authentic, and building genuine relationships. By investing in these activities and demonstrating your expertise and care for others, you can expand your network and attract clients who appreciate your dedication and professionalism.

Real estate is indeed a relationship-driven business, and trust and authenticity are key factors in building a successful career regardless of one's age, race, or personal history. Building strong relationships based on trust and genuine care is vital for establishing yourself as a reliable and reputable real estate professional.

Here are a few additional points to consider:

Effective Communication: Clear and honest communication fosters trust with your clients. Listen actively, understand their needs, and provide transparent information throughout the buying or selling process. Promptly address any concerns or questions they have to demonstrate your commitment to their best interests.

Professionalism and Expertise: Continually develop your knowledge and skills in the real estate industry. Stay updated on market trends, regulations, and best practices. By being knowledgeable and professional in your interactions, clients will perceive you as a trusted advisor and expert in your field.

Personal Branding: Establishing a strong personal brand helps differentiate you from competitors. Define your unique value proposition and communicate it across various channels. Your personal brand should align with your values, expertise, and the level of service you provide. This consistency builds trust and recognition among potential clients.

Referral and Repeat Business: Satisfied clients are more likely to refer you to their network or engage your services again in the future. Prioritize building lasting relationships by providing exceptional service, maintaining regular contact, and demonstrating your ongoing commitment to their success.

Going the Extra Mile: Show genuine care for your clients by going above and beyond their expectations. Offer personalized service, provide valuable insights, and assist with additional resources beyond the transaction itself. This level of care fosters trust and creates a positive experience, which increases the likelihood of repeat business and referrals.

Building trust and authenticity takes time. Focus on developing meaningful connections, delivering exceptional service, and continuously nurturing your relationships. By doing so, you can build a successful real estate business that transcends personal attributes and reflects your dedication to providing exceptional value to your clients.

Real estate is a relationship business. If you put yourself in situations where you build trust, you hold the key to building your business.

CHAPTER TWO
Wrestling the Myth Beast

"One deal does not a career make."
—Tracy McLaughlin, Realtor

CHAPTER SUMMARY
In this chapter, I shared part of my journey of entering the real estate commission business with no goals, business plan, or clients. I underlined the importance of understanding the financial involvement of starting a commission-based business. I dispelled common myths about the profession and provided tips on how to get started on building a successful career in real estate. I emphasized the value of having a financial cushion, being a good money manager, and having the flexibility to be available for your clients. I finally discussed the importance of networking, building relationships, and providing value to clients without pressuring them.

REVIEW
Here is a summary of the common myths of having a real estate career:

Myth #1: *There will be consistent and immediate cash flow.* Embarking on a new business, particularly in real estate, involves grappling with the myth of immediate and consistent cash flow. In reality, monthly broker and association fees, in addition to various expenses such as marketing, transportation, MLS and local board fees, can put you in a negative financial position.

Myth #2: *A career in real estate offers flexibility in terms of setting your own hours.*
Contrary to the belief that real estate offers flexible hours, it actually requires agents to be readily available and flexible to meet the needs of clients who may also juggle complex schedules. On top of balancing personal commitments with the demands of the real estate industry, agents must also dedicate time to brand and business development.

Myth #3: *Knowing a lot of people automatically translates into having a lot of clients.*
Despite having close relationships, some may not choose to use your services, and you must respect their decisions. Friends and family do not owe you their business. Building a robust network takes time, authenticity, and genuine effort; you must provide value, demonstrate your expertise, and build meaningful relationships to attract the right kind of clients.

REFLECTION QUESTIONS
1. What financial and practical preparations will you need to make before starting a commission-based business such as real estate?
2. What are some networking opportunities you can explore? How can you develop the right kind of relationships to grow your business?
3. How can you use your skills and interests to provide value to your clients without directly asking for their business?

SCENARIOS
Scenario 1: You just started your real estate career, but you're having trouble balancing your personal life and professional commitments. What can you do to ensure you're available for your clients without sacrificing your personal life?

Scenario 2: Your friends and family aren't hiring you as their real estate agent. How can you continue to build your business without relying on them for support?

TO-DO LIST
- Research different brokerage models and fees to determine the best fit for your real estate goals.
- Develop a financial plan, including a budget and a cushion, for your first few months in the real estate business.
- Create a daily schedule that sets aside time for business-building activities and client meetings.
- Identify networking opportunities in your community and attend events to expand your professional network. Start by looking into events and organizations in your area. List some of those findings below.

STEP-BY-STEP INSTRUCTIONS
- Read the chapter and take notes.
- Reflect on the questions provided and write down your responses.
- Complete the to-do list.
- Reflect on your goals from Chapter 1. Write down new ones or adjust your existing goals (if you feel you need to).

TIPS AND TAKEAWAYS
- Be prepared for inconsistent income and financial challenges when starting a commission-based business.
- Be flexible and available for your clients by adjusting your schedule to accommodate their needs.
- Build relationships with potential clients by providing value without pressuring them for business.
- Continually develop your knowledge and skills in the real estate industry.

- Establish a strong personal brand to differentiate you from competitors.

Your own tips and takeaways:

- _____
  _____
- _____
  _____
- _____
  _____

CHAPTER THREE
Are You Made For This Business?

"You don't build a business, you build people,
then people build the business."
—Zig Ziglar

In the journey of building a business or reinventing an existing one, it is crucial to understand your purpose and identify your "why" in the universe. Without clarity on these aspects, it becomes challenging to know where to begin. Research has shown that individuals who grasp their why are more likely to embrace challenges and adapt quickly.

The foundation upon which you build your business is paramount and directly linked to its long-term success. If you lack clarity about who you are and the path you are taking, your foundation becomes akin to a crumbling cinder block base without concrete fill. It might appear appealing from the outside, but it will not support the weight of future additions or modifications. Like a foundation, your business requires a solid base.

While reading this chapter and reflecting on its contents, do not allow someone else's perception of you define who you are. At some point in our lives, many of us have become the version of ourselves that others want us to be, with the intention of providing them with happiness or security. If you have spent your life molding yourself into the cumulative expectations of others, the person you are projecting and existing as may not truly reflect your authentic self.

So, who are you?

Discovering your true identity and purpose is a journey of self-reflection and introspection. It involves peeling away the layers of external expectations and societal pressures to reveal the essence of your being. It requires courage to acknowledge and embrace your passions, values, and strengths, even if they differ from what others expect of you.

Take time to explore your interests, engage in activities that ignite your enthusiasm, and seek out experiences that challenge and stretch your abilities. Reflect on your values and beliefs, understanding what truly resonates with you at a fundamental level. It is through this process that you will uncover the person you are destined to become.

Remember the words of Ralph Waldo Emerson: "The only person you are destined to become is the person you decide to be." Embrace the power of choice and take ownership of your path. Align your personal values with your business aspirations and create a harmonious connection that will guide your decisions and actions.

Ultimately, being true to yourself and embracing your unique identity will not only bring you fulfillment but also attract like-minded individuals to your business. Your authenticity will resonate with others and create a genuine connection that fosters trust and loyalty.

Indeed, only you can determine if you are made for the real estate business. It requires a deep understanding of your purpose, values, and motivations. Take time to reflect on what drives you, what brings you joy, and what you envision for your life and career. Consider your strengths, passions, and areas of expertise that you can leverage in the real estate industry.

Being successful in real estate requires perseverance, resilience, and a genuine desire to serve others. It involves building relationships, navigating challenging conversations, and continuously adapting to market conditions. Assess whether you possess the necessary skills and qualities to thrive in this dynamic and people-oriented field.

Embrace your authentic self in any business, including real estate. Clients look for real estate professionals who are genuine, trustworthy, and relatable. Being true to yourself not only attracts the right clients but also brings more fulfillment to your work. Find ways to incorporate your unique strengths, values, and personality into your business practices. Let your authenticity shine through your interactions, marketing efforts, and overall approach to serving clients.

Embarking on a real estate career that aligns with who you truly are ensures that you find meaning and fulfillment in your work. It allows you to bring your best self to the table, connect deeply with clients, and make a positive impact in their lives. Success in real estate is not solely measured by financial achievements but also by the satisfaction and purpose you derive from your work.

Before making a decision, explore and educate yourself about the real estate industry. Speak with other professionals in the field, attend industry events, and conduct thorough research. Seek guidance from mentors or coaches who can provide valuable insights and support as you embark on this journey.

Ultimately, only you can answer whether you are made for the real estate business. Trust your instincts, follow your passion, and be willing to put in the effort and commitment required to succeed. With the right mindset, continuous learning, and a genuine desire to serve, you can build a fulfilling and successful career in real estate.

For a significant portion of my life, I was in survival mode, merely going through the motions without truly living my why.

In all honesty, I was not even aware that having a why was important. I had children, and being a mother meant I had the responsibility to support them. This led me to realize that I needed a job to provide for my family, and to increase my income to better support them, I worked hard and sought promotions. The why seemed obvious. Or so I thought.

It is understandable that, in the midst of the responsibilities and demands of everyday life, we often focus on fulfilling immediate needs and responsibilities without considering our deeper purpose or why. I believe many people find themselves in a similar situation where they prioritize survival and practicality over personal fulfillment. Discovering and living your why can bring a sense of purpose and fulfillment to your life. It involves understanding your values, passions, and what truly matters to you on a deeper level. Your why can guide your decisions, actions, and the way you live your life.

Reflecting on your current situation and the path you have taken is an important first step. It is commendable that you recognized the need to provide for your family, worked hard to seek advancement, and improved your income. It is also essential to reassess and evaluate whether your current trajectory aligns with your deeper sense of purpose and fulfillment.

Consider asking yourself some introspective questions:

- What are the things that truly matter to you in life?
- What are your passions, interests, and values?
- Are you currently living in alignment with those passions and values?
- What kind of impact do you want to have on your family, community, or the world?
- How can you incorporate your passions and values into your work and daily life?

Exploring these questions can help you gain clarity on your why and provide a starting point for making changes in your life. It might involve exploring the pursuit of personal goals and interests, or finding ways to integrate your passions into your business.

Discovering and living your why is a continuous process. It can evolve and change as you gain new experiences and insights. It is never too late to realign your life with your purpose and start living a more fulfilling and meaningful existence.

When we grapple with low self-esteem or an undefined purpose, it is nearly impossible to believe that we deserve the life we envision or even imagine the life we truly deserve. Dr. Brené Brown, in her book The Gifts of Imperfection, writes, "Don't shrink. Don't puff up. Stand your sacred ground."

These words hold relevance in various aspects of my personal life, and they can also be applied to numerous conversations and negotiations. But for now, let's focus on ourselves. Take a moment, close your eyes, and stay with me.

Don't shrink, don't puff up, and stand your sacred ground. Stand in the space that belongs solely to you.

Imagine spreading your wings as high and wide as they can reach. Where do you see yourself? Are you atop a towering building? Is the sky above you filled with gray clouds, or is the sun shining so brightly that you have to squint? Are you alone or surrounded by the people you hold dear? Are they attentively listening to you? Do they appear happy?

For this exercise, assume you are standing in the middle of a vibrant forest. The sun is radiating its brilliance and you are encircled by your closest friends and family. Familiar faces are in the circle, although you may not recall their names. Everyone in the circle is happy. Smiles adorn their faces. They are eager to know what message you have for them.

How do you feel?

Take a deep breath to allow the air to fill your lungs completely.

In this sacred space within your heart and mind, imagine what you have said or done to inspire the people standing beside you. You receive nods of approval and perhaps even a resounding applause. While the response is positive, you see emotions pent up in those assured by only the notion that you have truly done your best.

The sentiment you currently experience embodies your profound purpose. It prompts contemplation on the essential principles, dialogues, concessions, and sentiments that engender contentment, trust, and elation within your social sphere.

Understanding these elements signifies that you comprehend the kind of individual you aspire to be in every facet of your business endeavors as well as in your personal existence.

As you unravel your purpose and construct the bedrock upon which your entrepreneurial endeavors shall be erected, I implore you to steadfastly grasp this profound sensation and embrace the array of emotions that envelop it.

In times when your trajectory falters or adversities loom before you, I implore you to retreat to this sacred juncture, to the depths of that profound fulfillment and connectedness you once apprehended. Permit it to serve as an unwavering beacon, igniting the fervor of your resolve and rekindling the awareness of the influence you hold over the lives of those around you.

Remember, your why is unique to you. It is the driving force that propels you forward, empowering you to make a difference and create a meaningful existence. Embrace it, cherish it, and let it shape your journey as you build your business and lead a life aligned with your authentic self.

The next step in understanding your why is to reflect on where you came from, where you are currently, and where you want to be. This reflection helps you connect the dots and identify the change you want to create in the world through your business.

You might question how this reflection is relevant to selling real estate. After all, isn't the desire to sell real estate reason enough to get into the business and build on it? The easy answer is yes, but the correct answer is no.

Your why should go beyond the surface level of financial gain. It should delve into the impact you want to have on others, the sense of fulfillment you seek, and the legacy you want to leave behind.

Over time, I found that my why evolved. Initially, it was driven by the need to support my family, but as I grew and gained clarity, my why expanded. Today, my why includes coaching new agents and witnessing their growth, making a positive impact in people's lives through real estate education, and attaining financial stability.

Your why can encompass a multitude of elements, but dig deeper and explore all aspects of your life and how building a commission-based business will affect and change them. When you reach beyond the financial aspect of your why, you might discover a passion for connecting with new people, educating them, and positively influencing their lives through real estate transactions.

Perhaps you have an innate desire to be more connected to your community and real estate provides an avenue to fulfill that purpose. By exploring these aspects, you can infuse more meaning into your why and find greater fulfillment in your business.

Without clear goals, many enthusiastic new agents burn out and eventually leave the industry. They lack direction and fail to set specific, defined goals. Be clear about your goals and move beyond vague aspirations like "making $100,000" without a defined plan of action. Consider the sacrifices you need to make to achieve your goals and envision what your life will look like once you reach them.

To enhance your goal-setting process, write a letter from your future self. Visualize where you want to be in one year and reflect on your accomplishments, failures, and lessons learned, both personally and professionally. This exercise allows you to set intentions and consider the actions required to achieve your envisioned future. Revisit this letter regularly to keep your intentions and goals in focus.

Breaking down your goals into different categories is a powerful way to ensure that you have a well-rounded and balanced approach to your personal and professional growth. Here are four categories you can use to set your goals: personal, financial, dream big, and self-improvement.

Personal Goals are centered around personal well-being and growth. They can include physical health, mental and emotional well-being, relationships, and personal development. Examples of personal goals may include:

- Losing 10 pounds and maintaining a healthy lifestyle.
- Practicing mindfulness and meditation for 15 minutes every day.
- Strengthening relationships by spending quality time with loved ones.
- Reading at least one book per month to expand your knowledge and perspective.
- Taking regular breaks and vacations to recharge and enjoy life outside of work.

Financial Goals focus on financial growth and stability. They can include targets for income, savings, investments, and debt reduction. Examples of financial goals may include:

- Increasing your annual income by a specific percentage or dollar amount.
- Saving a certain amount of money each month or establishing an emergency fund.
- Investing in real estate properties or other income-generating assets.
- Paying off credit card debt or reducing overall debt by a certain amount.
- Creating a budget and tracking expenses to achieve financial discipline.

Dream-Big Goals allow you to unleash your imagination and aim for extraordinary achievements. Dream-big goals are about stretching beyond your comfort zone and pursuing ambitious aspirations. Examples of dream-big goals may include:

- Starting your own real estate brokerage or expanding your existing business.
- Owning a luxury property in a desirable location.
- Becoming a renowned expert or thought leader in your field.

- Contributing to charitable causes or establishing a philanthropic foundation.
- Traveling the world and experiencing different cultures and landscapes.

Self-Improvement Goals focus on personal growth and continuous self-improvement that cover various aspects of your life such as skills development, mindset, and self-awareness. Examples of self-improvement goals may include:

- Enhancing your negotiation and communication skills through training or workshops.
- Cultivating a positive mindset and practicing gratitude daily.
- Building resilience and learning to manage stress effectively.
- Developing leadership skills and becoming an influential mentor to others.
- Pursuing ongoing education or certification to stay updated in your field.

Once you identify your goals in each category, write them down. Putting your goals into writing solidifies your intentions and helps you stay accountable. You can create a personal goal-setting journal or use digital tools and apps to track your progress.

While pursuing your primary business goal, such as selling 35 homes, take time to celebrate the small victories along the way. Recognize and reward yourself for each home sale, as these accomplishments contribute to your overall success. Treat yourself to something special for every milestone reached, whether it's buying a new outfit, indulging in a spa day, or taking a mini-vacation.

Celebrating your wins not only boosts your motivation and confidence but also fosters a positive mindset that will help you navigate challenges and setbacks.

Remember that goal setting is an ongoing process. Regularly review and adjust your goals as you progress and as your priorities evolve. By maintaining a balanced approach and nurturing all aspects of your life, you will achieve success in your real estate career and experience personal fulfillment and growth.

Building a successful business in real estate requires more than just technical knowledge and skills; it demands a deep understanding of your purpose and motivations. By uncovering your why, you can tap into a source of inspiration and drive that will propel you forward even in the face of obstacles.

Once you have identified your why, develop a clear and actionable plan to bring it to life. Set specific goals in different areas of your life, including personal, financial, dream big, and self-improvement. Break down these goals into smaller, manageable steps and commit to being consistent in your efforts. Consistency is the key that will turn your goals into reality.

Throughout your journey, remember that real estate is a relationship business. It is not solely about buying and selling properties; it is about serving and connecting with people. How you conduct yourself under pressure, manage your clients' stress, and provide honest advice and market knowledge will define your reputation and ultimately lead to your success.

Embrace the power of consistency in your marketing efforts. Whether it is door-to-door knocking, delivering flyers, or nurturing client relationships, commit to doing it consistently. Building a strong foundation takes time and effort, but with consistency, you will see the fruits of your labor.

Invest in your personal growth by understanding your strengths and weaknesses. Consider taking personality tests to gain insights into your unique characteristics and preferences. Use this self-awareness to tailor your marketing strategies, improve your communication skills, and identify areas where you may need additional support.

Your why should extend beyond just making money. Find joy and fulfillment in helping people achieve their dreams and guiding them through important financial decisions. When you prioritize serving others and providing value, the financial rewards will naturally follow.

Stay self-motivated throughout your real estate journey. While you may receive support from your broker and colleagues, ultimately, your success depends on your internal drive and determination. Stay focused, organized, and committed to taking action toward your goals.

As you embark on your real estate career, stay true to yourself and your purpose. Your why will be the guiding force that keeps you aligned with your goals and helps you navigate challenges along the way. Embrace the journey, embrace personal growth, and let your why lead you to a fulfilling and successful career in real estate.

It is not enough to engage in sporadic marketing activities or make occasional connections with potential clients. Consistency means committing to regular and ongoing efforts to nurture relationships, provide value, and stay top-of-mind with your target audience.

When it comes to marketing initiatives like delivering donuts to mortgage brokers, understand that one-time efforts will not yield significant results. Consistently diarizing these deliveries and making them a monthly task will help you build familiarity and rapport with the brokers. Additionally, going beyond the simple act of delivering donuts by following up with phone calls and genuinely showing interest in their needs and challenges will foster stronger connections and open opportunities for collaboration.

Consistency extends beyond marketing activities. It applies to all aspects of your business, including client communication, lead generation, networking, and self-improvement. By consistently showing up and delivering on your promises, you establish trust and reliability, which are vital in the real estate industry.

Consider implementing these strategies to maintain consistency in your business:

Time Management and Planning: Use effective time management techniques to allocate specific time blocks to take care of your business tasks. Plan your days and weeks in advance, setting aside dedicated periods for lead generation, client communication, administrative tasks, and self-improvement activities. By having a clear plan, you ensure that you consistently make progress toward your goals.

Customer Relationship Management: Use a customer relationship management (CRM) system to track and manage your client interactions. Regularly follow up with leads, current clients, and past clients to nurture those relationships over time. Consistently provide value by sharing relevant information, market updates, and personalized recommendations based on their needs and preferences.

Self-Motivation and Accountability: Realize that as a real estate professional, you are essentially self-employed. You must be self-motivated and hold yourself accountable for your actions and results. Set clear goals, track your progress, and regularly assess your performance. Celebrate your successes, learn from your challenges, and consistently strive for improvement.

Consistency is not about perfection, but rather making a commitment to showing up, even when faced with obstacles or setbacks. Through this effort you build trust, credibility, and long-term relationships that form the foundation of a successful real estate business.

If, for example, you decide to focus on area farming as a key element of your marketing plan, commit to attending specific activities over a significant period. Area farming involves targeting a specific geographic area and becoming a prominent presence within that community. To achieve this, you may engage in activities such as door knocking, delivering flyers, supporting local businesses, and placing permanent signage, and remember that results from area farming do not happen overnight.

By committing to regular door knocking and flyer distribution, you establish familiarity with the residents and demonstrate your dedication to serving the community. Additionally, supporting local businesses strengthens relationships and shows your investment in the local economy. These efforts contribute to building a positive reputation and brand recognition in the area.

Consistency is particularly critical in the early stages of area farming. It takes time for people to recognize and trust you; therefore, you must carry out these activities for at least a full year before you can expect tangible returns. You are building relationships and planting seeds that will gradually grow and bear fruit over time.

In my personal experience, breaking down goals and implementing consistent actions in my marketing plan and client management led to significant business growth. I achieved some success in my first year but encountered challenges in the second. In my third year I sought the guidance of a professional coach to develop a comprehensive business and marketing plan.

With the support of a coach and by consistently implementing the strategies outlined in my plan, I witnessed remarkable growth in my business. The consistent execution of marketing initiatives, client nurturing, and the establishment of clear systems and processes helped me double my business within a year.

As we move forward in the upcoming chapters, we will explore in more detail how to build an effective marketing plan tailored to your values, specific goals, and target audience. Regardless of the strategies you choose, consistency will be the driving force behind your success.

The act of doing the same tasks repeatedly is not just about following a rigid routine, but also about staying committed to your vision and goals, persistently taking action, and adapting when necessary. Through consistent efforts, day after day, week after week, and month after month, you will see sustainable growth in your real estate business.

Stay dedicated, be patient, and keep the long-term perspective in mind. With consistent and strategic efforts, you will pave the way for success and achieve your business goals.

Gaining self-awareness is a valuable asset in building your real estate business. If you find it difficult to see yourself objectively or identify your strengths and weaknesses, personality tests can be a helpful resource. These tests provide insights into your personality traits, preferences, and behavioral tendencies, allowing you to better understand yourself and how you interact with others.

Several free online tests are available, such as the Myers-Briggs Type Indicator, 16Personalities, and DiSC assessments. These tests categorize individuals into different personality types based on various dimensions, such as extroversion/introversion, thinking/feeling, or dominant behavioral styles.

Taking these tests offers a starting point for self-reflection and provide insights into your personality, communication style, and work preferences. While free tests provide some general insights, investing in detailed assessments may offer a more comprehensive understanding of your strengths and weaknesses. These assessments often provide in-depth reports and analysis, offering a clearer picture of your unique personality traits, motivators, and areas for improvement. Working with a certified professional or coach who specializes in these assessments can provide further guidance and interpretation of the results.

Understanding your personality and strengths can help you determine how to market effectively yourself by aligning your marketing strategies with your natural tendencies and capitalizing on your unique strengths. For example, if you are an extroverted and sociable person, you may excel at networking events and leveraging your interpersonal skills to build connections. If you have a detail-oriented and analytical personality, you may focus more on data-driven marketing strategies and showcasing your expertise through market analyses and statistics.

Moreover, self-awareness can transform your approach to developing your business plan and creating efficiencies. Recognizing your strengths helps you leverage them in areas where you excel, while understanding your weaknesses can guide you in seeking support or improving those areas. By aligning your business plan with your personality traits and strengths, you can design systems and processes that complement your natural inclinations and enhance your productivity.

Effective communication is crucial in real estate, and self-awareness plays a significant role in this aspect as well. Understanding your communication style and preferences allows you to adapt your messaging and approach to effectively connect with clients and prospects. If you know that you struggle with difficult conversations, you can develop strategies and scripts to navigate challenging situations more effectively. Similarly, if you excel at building relationships and connecting with others, you can focus on cultivating those skills in your interactions.

Personality tests are just one tool in gaining self-awareness. They provide insights, but they should be used as a starting point for reflection and personal growth. Building a successful real estate business requires ongoing self-improvement, adaptability, and a commitment to understanding yourself and your clients. Embrace the opportunity to learn more about yourself through these assessments and use that knowledge to develop strategies that align with your authentic self and drive your success in the real estate industry.

Navigating difficult conversations is also an integral part of the real estate business. It requires effective communication skills, confidence, and the ability to address challenging topics with professionalism and empathy. If you find yourself struggling with these types of conversations, particularly when it comes to pricing properties, you can employ strategies to approach them more effectively.

Preparation is key. Before engaging in a difficult conversation, take the time to gather relevant information and data that support your perspective. In the case of pricing a property, arm yourself with market statistics, comparable sales data, and any other relevant information that can help you explain and justify your pricing recommendations. This preparation will give you the confidence to address the client's unrealistic expectations right from the start.

Consider incorporating your strategies for addressing pricing concerns into your initial conversation with sellers or your listing presentation. By proactively discussing potential price reductions and outlining your planned approach, you demonstrate your expertise and commitment to achieving the best results for your clients. This sets the stage for open and honest communication throughout the transaction.

Approach these conversations from a place of authenticity and expertise. Be transparent with your clients about market realities and the factors influencing property values. Clearly articulate the risks and implications of overpricing, such as longer time on the market and potential price reductions down the line. Help clients understand the importance of setting a realistic price that aligns with current market conditions.

During these conversations, listen actively and empathetically to your clients' concerns and perspectives. Validate their emotions and show understanding while maintaining a professional stance. By actively listening, you can address their underlying needs and find common ground that leads to mutually beneficial solutions.

As a real estate professional, it is your responsibility to provide honest advice and guidance based on your expertise and market knowledge. While being empathetic and understanding is essential, it is equally important to assert your professional judgment when necessary. It's okay to respectfully challenge unrealistic expectations and guide clients toward more informed decisions.

Building strong relationships based on trust and open communication is key in successfully navigating these conversations. Demonstrating your commitment to serving clients' best interests and providing value will help them recognize you as a trusted advisor and expert in your field. This not only helps you acquire and retain business but also strengthens your reputation within the industry.

Engaging in a difficult conversation is an opportunity for growth and learning. Approach them with confidence, preparation, and a commitment to providing value to your clients. By honing your communication skills and standing your sacred ground, you can navigate these conversations effectively and ultimately contribute to the success of your real estate business.

Staying focused and on track is a common challenge in any business, including real estate. To overcome this challenge and maintain productivity, develop effective organizational strategies and systems that work for you.

One approach is to organize your calendar and allocate dedicated time blocks for business tasks. This helps create structure and ensures that you have designated periods to focus on specific activities. For example, you can block out time for lead generation, client communication, paperwork, market research, and self-improvement activities. By setting aside specific time slots for each task, you can better manage your workload and stay focused on completing them.

Find a system that works for you. Some real estate professionals prefer using digital calendars or productivity tools, such as Google Calendar or project management apps, to organize their schedules and tasks. These tools allow you to set reminders, prioritize tasks, and easily track your progress. Others may prefer traditional methods like physical planners or to-do lists. Experiment with different approaches and find the one that aligns with your preferences and helps you stay organized and focused.

In my experience, creating a daily to-do list has been effective in keeping me focused and productive. I prioritize tasks based on their urgency and importance and make sure to allocate time blocks for each task. As I complete each item on the list, I experience a sense of satisfaction and motivation, which helps me stay on track.

Real estate is a relationship business not solely focused on properties. How you conduct yourself under pressure and how you manage your clients' stress and concerns will significantly impact your success. Building and nurturing strong relationships gains client trust and loyalty.

In high-pressure situations, maintain professionalism, empathy, and effective communication skills. Listen actively to your clients' needs and concerns, and respond with understanding and reassurance. Being a calming presence during stressful moments can go a long way in building trust and solidifying your reputation as a reliable and compassionate real estate professional.

Developing strong relationships with clients requires consistent and proactive communication. Keep your clients informed about market updates, property showings, and any progress related to their real estate transactions. Regularly check in with them to see how they're doing and if they have any questions or concerns. By staying connected and engaged, you show your clients that their interests are your top priority.

Real estate is a people-centric industry, and the relationships you build contribute to your long-term success. By staying focused, organized, and dedicated to providing exceptional service, you can effectively manage your business tasks while nurturing strong relationships with your clients.

Knowing who you are and living your truth are important aspects of personal integrity and can greatly impact your overall well-being and future success. When you align your actions, values, and beliefs, both internally and externally, you create a sense of authenticity and congruence that can positively influence various areas of your life.

Here are some reasons why living your truth and embracing personal integrity are important:

Authenticity: Living your truth means being honest with yourself and others about your values, desires, and beliefs. When you are authentic, you attract genuine connections and build relationships based on trust and mutual understanding.

Inner Fulfillment: Embracing your true self and living in alignment with your values and passions brings a deep sense of fulfillment and satisfaction. It allows you to engage in activities and pursue goals that genuinely resonate with you, leading to a greater sense of purpose and contentment.

Self-Confidence: Knowing who you are and being true to yourself boosts self-confidence. When you embrace your uniqueness and live authentically, you develop a stronger sense of self-worth and self-assurance, which can positively impact various aspects of your life, including relationships, career, and personal growth.

Decision-Making: When you are clear about your values and personal truth, it becomes easier to make decisions that align with your authentic self. You can evaluate opportunities, choices, and challenges based on what truly matters to you, which leads to more informed and fulfilling decisions.

Inspiring Others: By living your truth, you become an inspiration to others. Your authenticity and integrity can motivate those around you to explore and embrace their own truths, creating a ripple effect of positive change and growth in your personal and professional circles.

Living your truth is a personal journey that requires self-reflection, self-acceptance, and the courage to be true to yourself, even when it may challenge societal expectations or norms. The ongoing process of self-discovery and growth leads to a more fulfilling and purposeful life.

When you learn you to harness the power that already exists inside of you, you open the world up to yourself and others.

CHAPTER THREE
Are You Made For This Business?

*"The only person you are destined to become
is the person you decide to be."*
—Ralph Waldo Emerson

CHAPTER SUMMARY

In this chapter, I discussed your "why"—your purpose in life and in business, and how knowing your why helps you overcome challenges more swiftly and easily. I challenged you to define yourself and not let someone else's vision of you dictate your identity. I advised you to clarify your goals and act upon your intentions, as well as to be prepared, organized, and focused. I highlighted the importance of standing your ground while remaining empathetic to your clients' perspectives, and of being an effective communicator. I reflected on the significance of living your truth with authenticity and integrity with the aim to inspire and motivate others. This can create a ripple effect of positive change and growth in your personal and professional circles.

REFLECTION QUESTIONS

1. Why do you think being in survival mode kept me from my why?
2. Do you feel you are made for this business? Why or why not? What motivates you? What are your challenges?
3. How does setting clear goals mitigate against burnout and giving up?

4. Take a moment to close your eyes and imagine yourself attaining your biggest dream. Where do you see yourself? Who is around you? What are they saying about you? How do you feel?

SCENARIOS

Scenario 1: Growing up you tried your hardest to please your family. You graduated college with a degree that doesn't inspire you and a lot of student debt. You feel stuck. You realize that you pursued a dream that wasn't your own. Go back in time and imagine telling yourself and your family your why and pursuing that instead. What would that be? How would that go?

Scenario 2: A client is pushing you to the brink. Their unrealistic expectations and reluctance to take your advice is making it nearly impossible to move forward. You know you must have a frank discussion with them in order to maintain your relationship. How do you navigate a difficult conversation with this client?

TO-DO LIST

- Write a personal mission statement. Define your purpose, your motivation and your why.
- What are your core values—the fundamental beliefs and priorities that drive you?
- Take a personality test (such as DiSC, Myers & Briggs, 16Personalities) List the strengths and weaknesses of your personality profile.
- Write a letter to your future self. Imagine where you will be when you reach your goals, both personally and professionally.
- Write down your goals–personal, financial, dream big, and self-invention. Next to each goal, write how you plan to action it. Give yourself a timeline, set reminders, and stick to it. Use the SMART method to help guide you (be Specific

about your goal, be sure it is Measurable, Attainable, Realistic, and can be completed in a Timely manner.)

Take your time with these exercises. This practice sets the foundation for your future self and business.

STEP-BY-STEP INSTRUCTIONS

- Read through the chapter, noting anything that stands out to you.
- Complete the reflection questions and scenarios.
- Work through the to-do list.
- Reflect on the results of your personality test and get a better understanding of your strengths and weaknesses.
- As you go through each exercise, envision your future self. Keep that vision foremost in your mind.
- Revisit your goals and the letter to your future self regularly.

TIPS AND TAKEAWAYS

- Be consistent. This is what will get you to your goals.
- Be very clear in stating your goals as opposed to making general, loose, or undefined goals.
- Do not let someone else's version of you define you.
- Seek guidance from mentors or coaches who provide valuable insights and support as you embark on this journey.
- Stand your ground. While it is essential to be empathetic and understanding, it is equally important to assert your professional judgment when necessary.

Your own takeaways:

- _____
  _____
- _____
  _____
- _____
  _____

CHAPTER FOUR
Who Will Buy a House from You?

"What you think, you become.
What you feel, you attract.
What you imagine, you create."
—Buddha

Once you have a clear understanding of your purpose and motivations for building a business, identifying your target audience or clientele is the next step in developing a successful business strategy. Understanding your audience helps you tailor your products, services, and marketing efforts to better meet their needs and preferences.

Some steps to help you identify your clientele include:
- Define your business identity based the values you discovered in the previous chapter.
- Conduct market research to gain insights into your local industry, competitors, and potential customer segments.
- Consider factors such as age, gender, location, interests, income level, and lifestyle.
- Envision the personas of your buyer clients so you can imagine and plan how you can best market that personality type to your target audience based on research, analysis, and your vision of what you want your business and daily interactions to look like.
- Identify the problems, needs, and pain points your target audience faces. How can you resolve these?

By following these steps, you create a strong foundation for your business and attract clients who align with your purpose and contribute to your success.

I reflect upon my early experiences in the real estate industry and the importance of setting intentions and goals. It is true that having a clear vision and aligning your values with your career can be powerful motivators.

Starting each year with a clean slate and working toward your goals can indeed be both exciting and daunting. The fear of starting from zero can serve as a driving force to push yourself and strive for success. As you gain experience and build your career, that excitement becomes intertwined with the thrill of meeting new people and helping them find their dream homes.

Reflect on your why and keep your values in focus throughout your career journey. Creating a vision board can be a helpful tool to visually represent your goals, aspirations, and the things that matter most to you. It serves as a reminder of what you are working toward and can be updated as your vision evolves.

Believing in yourself and your abilities is essential, even when facing challenges or when the path ahead seems difficult. While it may be challenging to envision who will buy property from you without having made a purchase yourself, remember that hard work, dedication, and continuous learning can overcome obstacles and turn what may seem impossible into possibilities.

By staying focused, setting clear intentions, and adapting to change, you can make progress toward your goals and achieve success in the real estate industry.

The characteristics of your ideal client evolve over time, so regularly revisit and update your understanding of your target audience. By doing so, you position yourself and your business in a way that attracts and resonates with your desired clientele.

Always be your best representation of yourself and you will meet people in the most unexpected and sometimes unassuming ways. I met a client who had sold a couple of properties with me and then purchased one through an interesting scenario. I was taking a trip with a girlfriend and a group of people from the gym I frequented early on in my real estate career. As we went through the airport security check, a security officer stopped me and asked if he could go through my bag. Not really having a choice if I wanted to continue to the terminal gate, I obliged.

As he went through my bag, I asked him if he was looking for anything in particular, to which he replied in a stoic voice, "Ma'am you have a knife in your purse." I laughed out loud and replied, "There is no way I have a knife in my purse." After rifling through my bag, he retrieved my keychain on which I had the office key I had just received from my broker. The key fob was attached to was a retractable knife. The security officer looked at me and advised me that he was going to have to confiscate the "knife" from me. I laughed and replied, "No problem at all. In fact, my office phone number is on the fob, so if you're thinking of buying or selling a property, give that number a call and I will be happy to assist you."

Six months later, my phone rang and I was meeting with the security officer to list his home. Since then, we have developed a friendship and we often reminisce about the security stop and have shared more than the occasional laugh over the incident.

It's amazing how chance encounters and unexpected situations can lead to meaningful connections and business opportunities. My interaction with the security officer at the airport turned out to be a serendipitous moment that led to a client relationship and a friendship.

This story highlights the importance of being open and receptive to opportunities in various aspects of your life, including chance encounters during travel or social activities.

Use every opportunity as a chance to showcase your professionalism and offer your services.

Building relationships and connections with people can happen in unexpected ways, and sometimes, it is those unique experiences that forge strong bonds. The fact that I developed a friendship with the security officer and later listed his home demonstrates the power of personal connections and the impact of positive interactions.

These types of anecdotes should remind us that being open and approachable and maintaining a positive attitude can lead to unexpected business opportunities and long-lasting relationships. It is a testament to the importance of building genuine connections and leaving a positive impression wherever you go.

I met another one of my long-term clients at an open house. I listed a property that was essentially a tear down, or a very large renovation project, in a familiar neighborhood. A middle-aged couple came through the open house and, after spending approximately fifteen minutes inside, they approached me and asked what I thought the property might be worth if it was fully renovated. To be transparent, this home had been neglected and was not an ideal property for an investor to renovate and resell for profit. The home had an awkward layout, the second-story ceilings were low, there was little to no curb appeal, and the basement took in water.

My response to the couple was that I did not see value in renovating this home for resale. The layout and low ceilings would not attract enough of a buyer pool for it to be profitable. Based on its location, it would be a solid investment to make some updates and hold as a rental. The home was priced at its lot value and, based on the opportunity to redevelop the land in the future, it would be worthwhile to hold. The couple then told me they had been working with another agent and were keenly interested in getting into the "flipping" business. They had never flipped a property before, but they had owned multiple properties and had a fairly large rental portfolio. They were knowledgeable on how to finance a property but not on the profitability or the process of renovating a property for immediate resale. The couple asked me about a property one street over that was on the market. They had already viewed the property and felt it might be a good project to start with.

I agreed to meet them at the second property the next day. From the living room and bedroom windows was a clear view of a main thoroughfare that supplies one of the transit hubs in our city. I said to the couple again that this was not a property that would make a lot of money because too many buyers would cross it off their list due to the busy street and the view.

I recommended that we visit a home nearby that I had previously shown and knew was vacant. We did a walk-through and wrote an offer that day. The couple became personal friends and have renovated and sold multiple properties with me. A year or two into our friendship, we got to talking about how we met and they advised me that they chose to work with me based solely on my honesty with them. I could have given them bad advice about the property we met in. After all, it was my listing and it would have meant double the paycheck I needed, but I gained a long-term client and a multitude of paychecks by showing up as my best self for their benefit.

This story serves as another example of how honesty and looking out for your clients' best interests can lead to long-term relationships and business success. By providing genuine and transparent advice about the properties they were interested in, I easily demonstrated my expertise and integrity, which resonated with the couple.

In the real estate industry, trust and credibility are paramount, and your willingness to prioritize clients' best interests over potential short-term gains make a lasting impression. By showing up as your best self and putting your clients' needs first, you will establish a strong foundation for a mutually beneficial relationships with the people you meet.

Becoming an expert in your area comes down to building trust with potential clients. By being knowledgeable and providing the information they seek, you establish yourself as a reliable source of expertise. This trust-building process begins by understanding the specific needs and priorities of your target audience.

For example, when hosting an open house for a large four-bedroom, two-story home in a suburban neighborhood, families attending the event will likely prioritize factors such as the quality of nearby schools, convenience of public transportation, and proximity to local community clubs. By proactively gathering and presenting this information, you demonstrate your understanding of their needs and showcase your commitment to meeting them where they are.

Equipping yourself with relevant resources is essential to being knowledgeable about the market in your area. You can access data on average sale prices, recent sales, and other market trends to provide your clients with valuable insights. This demonstrates your professionalism and positions you as an authority in the real estate industry.

Expertise is not determined solely by your age or length of time in the business. It is a combination of in-depth knowledge, continuous learning, and a commitment to staying up to date with market trends and changes. By staying informed, you can confidently answer clients' questions, offer sound advice, and provide guidance throughout the real estate process.

From the moment I entered the real estate business, I had a strong desire to focus on my beloved neighborhood. It held a special place in my heart, and I possessed intimate knowledge of its schools' quality, the diverse programs they offered, and the array of amenities provided by the community center. To maximize my opportunities, I eagerly embraced every chance to host open houses for fellow agents in the area. Armed with up-to-date information on recent sales, current listings, and upcoming properties or community developments, I ensured I was well-prepared for every interaction.

I made it a priority to personally view each new listing as soon as it hit the market. This way, I could confidently discuss the strengths, weaknesses, and unique aspects of each property that had recently been or was currently available. My volunteer work at the local school and my role on the community center's board further enriched my knowledge. I became well-versed in the range of programs offered at different schools and the variety of activities provided by the community center.

By immersing myself in these experiences, I established a comprehensive understanding of my neighborhood, making me a trusted resource for potential clients. In my inaugural year, I achieved remarkable success by listing and selling properties at a level equivalent to my direct competitors within this specific neighborhood.

This journey exemplifies the importance of focusing on a specific area of expertise. By dedicating myself to my neighborhood and actively participating in community initiatives, I gained an in-depth understanding of its offerings and became a go-to agent for individuals seeking guidance within that locale.

When I ventured into the world of real estate, I was fortunate to have already owned and renovated multiple homes. Additionally, many of my friends, who were primarily in their mid- to late-forties, were already homeowners. As a result, a significant portion of my early business originated directly from my social circle and their referrals.

If you find yourself in a different stage of life, you might think, "My friends don't have the financial means or the inclination to invest in real estate." This is a valid concern; however, your friends have their own networks, including colleagues, family members, and acquaintances, some of whom may be in a position to invest in real estate or are planning to move in the near future. Statistically speaking, most people move approximately every four years. So, for every person you know who has lived in their home for a decade, you likely know someone who will move 2.5 times within that same period.

This insight highlights the potential for expanding your client base beyond your immediate social circle. By nurturing relationships with friends and leveraging their connections, you can tap into a broader network of individuals who may be in the market for real estate services. Even if your friends are not your target clients, they still serve as valuable sources of referrals and introductions to potential clients.

Networking extends beyond personal friendships. Engaging in professional associations, attending industry events, and actively participating in online communities expands your reach and connects you with individuals who are actively involved in real estate or have an interest in investing. While your immediate social circle may not represent your primary client base, they play a role in facilitating connections and referrals, which leads to opportunities with individuals who have the financial capacity and intention to invest in real estate.

So, even if your friends don't fit the profile of potential clients, they can still be valuable assets in your network by helping you reach a wider audience and generate business through their referrals and connections.

When you deliver exceptional service, clients are more likely to share their positive experiences with others, akin to how gossip spreads. Word-of-mouth referrals can be incredibly powerful in the real estate industry. Satisfied clients who had a memorable experience will enthusiastically recommend your services to their friends, family, and acquaintances. This creates a ripple effect, expanding your network and attracting new clients.

Considering the average commission earned from each client throughout your career can amount to $100,000, it emphasizes the long-term value of consistently delivering exceptional service. Each client you serve with excellence becomes a potential source of referrals and future business opportunities. By showing up fully prepared, committed, and ready to win, you demonstrate your professionalism and dedication, further enhancing the likelihood of positive client experiences which equates to commissions earned and business growth.

Maintaining a mindset that every interaction is an opportunity to provide a memorable experience will set you apart from your competitors. Going above and beyond to exceed client expectations, offering personalized attention, and providing a smooth transaction process will leave a lasting impression. These positive experiences become the foundation for building strong relationships and generating a steady stream of referrals, which can significantly contribute to your success.

I recently initiated a mentorship program with two women in their early twenties. During our first session on identifying their sphere of influence, they expressed uncertainty about where to begin and whom to approach. One of them mentioned that her mother, who is currently renting, possessed the financial means for a down payment but was hesitant about taking on the responsibilities of homeownership. In response, I suggested that she propose to her mother the idea of utilizing those funds to purchase a rental property instead. By doing so, her mother could benefit from the income generated by someone else paying the mortgage while continuing to pay rent to her landlord. This approach would allow her to leverage someone else's income and experience a return on her investment without the day-to-day management responsibilities that come with owning a primary residence.

I emphasized the importance of choosing a stable market and a suburban area that maintains a relatively consistent performance over major cities that often see highs and lows. This selection would provide annual appreciation of the property and the advantage of having someone else contribute to the mortgage, accelerating the process of securing her retirement.

By presenting this alternative perspective, I aimed to encourage creative thinking and exploration of various investment opportunities within the real estate sector to enable these agents to have a broader perspective of who would buy a house from them.

There are several ways you can educate the general public on how to access funds or create savings for their real estate endeavors. One option is to explore the possibilities of withdrawing from a Registered Retirement Savings Plan (RRSP) or a Tax-Free Savings Account (TFSA). These government-incentivized programs provide opportunities for buyers to shift their savings without incurring penalties, enabling first-time homebuyers to enter the real estate market sooner than they might have anticipated.

Take it upon yourself to understand the programs available to your clients within the area where you live or work. Familiarize yourself with the local incentives and initiatives designed to support homebuyers. This knowledge will empower you to provide valuable guidance and advice to your clients so they can navigate the options that will free up funds or create savings for their real estate goals.

By staying up to date with the latest government programs, grants, or tax incentives in your region, you can inform your clients about potential opportunities they may not have been aware of. This demonstrates your expertise and commitment to their success and enhances your reputation as a knowledgeable and trusted real estate professional.

I have mentioned that if your friends do not buy houses from or with you, it may be time to seek out new connections. While this statement may initially sound harsh or even amusing, it holds a significant truth. If your current social circle lacks individuals who are interested in purchasing real estate or would not consider working with you, it becomes necessary to expand your network. This can be achieved by joining professional networking groups or actively engaging in door-to-door interactions to connect with people who are open to working with a real estate professional. By putting yourself in front of individuals who might be considering real estate transactions, you increase your chances of finding clients who are receptive to your services.

As people realize that you possess the knowledge and expertise to guide them smoothly from point A to point B, and provide the necessary information to make informed investment decisions, you become the vehicle that helps them achieve their goals. Whether they are investing for personal use, profit, or other investment purposes, your ability to deliver the desired outcomes will establish you as a trusted partner.

While it may require some effort and stepping outside of your comfort zone, expanding your social and professional circles is a big part of building a successful real estate career. Embracing networking opportunities, being proactive in seeking potential clients, and showcasing your expertise will position you as a go-to resource for individuals seeking guidance in their real estate endeavors.

The key is to foster relationships with people who value your knowledge and recognize the value you bring to the table. By actively seeking out connections with those interested in real estate, you increase your chances of finding clients who will appreciate and choose to work with you.

One of the most memorable clients I had the pleasure of working with came to me through Twitter. Frustrated and unable to envision how he and his wife could afford a home, he expressed his concerns in a tweet. Intrigued by his situation, I arranged a meeting with them to delve deeper into their financial circumstances.

During our meeting, I discovered that they had good credit, stable income, and minimal debt relative to their earnings. Recognizing their potential, I recommended that they visit their bank to explore the possibility of obtaining a line of credit. If they could manage both the line of credit payments and a mortgage, they would be able to afford their dream home.

Following my advice, they met with their lender and were approved for a line of credit that would cover the down payment and closing costs of the property. I advised them to transfer the line of credit balance into their savings account. Within 90 days, they were well-positioned to purchase a home, and they seized the opportunity by acquiring a charming, recently renovated bungalow in a delightful neighborhood. This took 90 days because that money had to stay in a savings or checking account that long in order for it to be considered savings opposed to money borrowed from a line of credit.

Not only did they become homeowners, but they also discovered that their mortgage, tax, and utility costs were lower than their previous rent payments. This realization brought them a sense of accomplishment and financial stability. Fast forward a few years and I had the honor of being the "best man" at the client's second wedding. He explained that choosing me for this role was natural because I had changed his life and helped him achieve a dream he had never thought possible.

It was a humbling experience to witness the profound impact that equipping someone with the necessary tools and knowledge for property ownership can have on their life. This encounter transformed his life and had a profound effect on mine. It reinforced the significance of my role as a real estate professional and ability to positively influence the lives of others.

This heartwarming journey serves as a reminder of the transformative power that real estate can have and the joy that comes from helping others realize their dreams of homeownership.

Fortunately, when I entered the real estate business, I had the advantage of previous business and real estate knowledge and experience. Surprisingly, my age did not impact my business growth as much as the lack of knowledge would have. Looking in the mirror and thinking of oneself as "just a kid" is common; however, I can confidently say that people over 45 have no inherent ability to gauge your age unless you give them the space to do so. Perception is what shapes reality.

Dispel the notion that age can inhibit your ability to achieve success. I assure you that as a "younger" agent, you likely possess a level of energy that surpasses my own. While you may be less experienced directly in real estate, recognize the unique assets and value you bring to potential buyers and sellers. Your energy is contagious, and your expertise in social media and web savviness can be leveraged to enhance your branding and marketing strategies. By utilizing these platforms, you effectively showcase your strengths and attract clients who resonate with your style.

What you put out into the world is what you will attract. Age is merely a number and not a definition of your abilities or potential for success in this business. You are the definition of yourself, regardless of the numerical value that represents the time you have spent on Earth. In real estate, there is no such thing as being too young or too old. Excelling in the industry is about utilizing your unique qualities, skills, and knowledge.

No matter what stage of life you are in when entering the world of commission sales, you must know your strengths, messaging, and how you can best serve your clients. In my case, I leveraged my knowledge and experience in renovating and flipping houses to build a strong referral base and establish my value proposition in the minds of potential clients.

By demonstrating my understanding of construction processes and highlighting potential issues to look out for, I continuously built trust with clients. Discussing modifications and improvements that can enhance resale value became a valuable aspect of my service. This expertise proved invaluable to clients, as they appreciated the insights and guidance I provided.

Moreover, I extended my value proposition beyond discussions by offering clients access to my trusted list of tradespeople. This ensured that they connected with reliable and honest professionals whom I had personally worked with for many years. I prioritized the establishment of this network of trusted partners because I considered my referral sources an extension of myself. I wanted my clients to experience the same level of reliability and integrity in all aspects of their real estate journey.

Interestingly, connecting my clients with my preferred partners also had a reciprocal benefit. Many of these tradespeople became my clients as well, as business relationships tend to be reciprocal in nature. This mutual support and collaboration strengthened my overall business, creating a network of trust and referrals.

In commission sales, building and nurturing relationships are vital. By utilizing your expertise, providing value-added services, and establishing a network of reliable partners, you create a thriving and reciprocal business environment. Ultimately, offering exceptional service and fostering reciprocal connections will contribute to the growth and success of your real estate career.

In his book *12 Power Principles for Success*, the late Bob Proctor emphasized that success is a path you deliberately choose. It is not determined by your financial status, age, identity, past achievements, or current circumstances. Success is about the direction you decide to take in your life, and it ultimately comes down to your choices. I strongly urge you to choose wisely.

Now, let's consider the question: Who will buy a house from you? The answer is simple: anyone who recognizes the value you bring. When you offer something of value to your clients, whether it is your expertise, guidance, or exceptional service, those who perceive the worth in what you provide will be eager to work with you.

The key lies in understanding and communicating the unique value proposition you bring to the table. By demonstrating your knowledge, professionalism, and commitment to your clients' success, you will attract clients who appreciate and recognize the benefits of working with you. Regardless of their background, age, or financial situation, those who see the value in what you offer will be the ones interested in buying a house from you.

CHAPTER FOUR
Who Will Buy a House from You?

*"Who will buy a house from you?
The answer is simple: anyone who
recognizes the value you bring."*
—**Marcia Bergen**

CHAPTER SUMMARY
In this chapter, I delved into the essence of succeeding in real estate by emphasizing the importance of understanding your purpose and identifying your audience to provide tailored services. I shared personal stories to underscore the value of honesty, trust, and expertise in building strong client relationships. I discussed the benefits of immersing yourself in your community and becoming a trusted resource for potential clients. I stressed the role of networking and consistent delivery of exceptional service, noting that even non-prospective clients in your social circle can offer valuable referrals. I also guided new agents on navigating their sphere of influence and educating potential clients on investment opportunities and government programs. I concluded the chapter by reaffirming that success is not determined by external circumstances but by your choices and the value you bring to others.

REFLECTION QUESTIONS
1. Can you think of a time when being open and approachable led to unexpected opportunities? How did that experience shape your perspective?

2. How can you better identify and understand your target audience? What steps can you take to cater to their needs and preferences more effectively?

3. Why is it important to maintain a mindset that every interaction is a potential opportunity?

4. What are some ways that you can leverage your personal network to grow your client base?

SCENARIOS

Scenario 1: A potential client you just met expressed a concern that you are perhaps too young or inexperienced to entrust with their portfolio. How would you respond?

Scenario 2: A client is interested in buying a rental property in a neighborhood that you are not too familiar with. After some research, you discover that there are several neighboring houses slated for demolition, and that there will be significant roadwork in addition to new construction projects over the next several years. How would you handle the situation?

CHAPTER FIVE
Who is Your Real Estate Personality?

*"We are not perfect human beings,
nor do we have to pretend to be,
but it is necessary for us to be the
best versions of ourselves we can be."*
—Satsuki Shibuya

Creating a clear and intentional perception of who you want to be in the real estate business is vital, as it sets the stage for attracting the clients you desire. A key aspect of achieving this is to develop the ability to meet people where they are in their journey in a way that resonates with and is relatable to them. This is a non-negotiable skill that allows you to create meaningful connections and provide tailored experiences for individuals at various stages of their lives.

Understanding that people's circumstances and needs can vary greatly, you must adapt your approach and appearance accordingly. Whether someone is going through a challenging time or experiencing a period of success, your job is to empathize, listen, and provide relevant support. By meeting them at their level, you demonstrate your genuine care and commitment to their unique situation.

At times, you will encounter clients who are facing obstacles or struggling with financial limitations. In these instances, your role is to provide guidance, explore alternative options, and offer solutions that align with their circumstances. By empathetically addressing their concerns and working collaboratively to find viable solutions, you establish trust and credibility.

Conversely, there will also be clients who are in a strong position, ready to make significant investments or take advantage of favorable market conditions. In such cases, your role shifts to being an expert advisor and providing insights and opportunities that align with their goals and aspirations. By leveraging your market knowledge and expertise, you can help these clients make informed decisions and seize lucrative opportunities.

Adapting your approach and mindset to meet clients at different levels is a powerful tool for building connections and establishing a strong reputation in the industry. It allows you to create an experience that resonates with individuals, making them more likely to choose you as their trusted real estate professional.

Every interaction is an opportunity to demonstrate your commitment to meeting people where they are at. By truly understanding their needs, concerns, and aspirations, you can offer tailored solutions and support. This ability to connect on a deeper level attracts the clients you desire and fosters long-lasting relationships built on trust and mutual understanding.

To attract the clients you want, establish who you want to be perceived as in the industry. Once you establish your identity and identify your target clients, the next step is to carefully consider how you want to be perceived by both your clients and the public. This perception attracts business and builds you a strong reputation in the industry.

Recognize that how you conduct yourself in business may differ from how you behave in your personal life. While you may have a different demeanor when enjoying time with your family or socializing with friends, professionalism and a focused approach are vital when dealing with real estate transactions.

Real estate transactions involve significant financial investments and, for most people, buying or selling a property is one of the largest transactions they will undertake. As their real estate professional, you must understand and empathize with the stress and pressure clients may experience throughout the process. Your role is to provide guidance, alleviate concerns, and navigate challenges on their behalf.

Managing and deflating stress is a required skill for continued success in the real estate industry. By maintaining a calm and composed demeanor, actively listening to your clients' concerns, and providing reassurance and expert advice, you help alleviate their anxieties. Effective communication and visual transparency in addressing potential issues or setbacks will further contribute to easing their stress.

Establishing a reputation as a reliable and trustworthy professional requires delivering exceptional service and maintaining a high level of professionalism. This includes being punctual, responsive, and attentive to your clients' needs. Building long-term relationships and generating referrals rely on your ability to build trust and demonstrate your commitment to their success.

I am not suggesting you create a persona that is detached from your authentic self; however, it is beneficial to establish boundaries and maintain a level of separation between your personal life and your business persona. For example, people are aware that I have a golden doodle that occasionally accompanies me to the office, I am a proud grandmother, or that I have a passion for interior design and have renovated multiple houses. These aspects are true and accurate, but they do not encompass the entirety of how I show up visually as a professional.

To effectively guide your clients and ensure they understand that you have their best interests at heart, project a focused and knowledgeable image. This is the impression that will resonate with them and leave a lasting impression.

Maintaining professional boundaries does not mean hiding or denying your personal interests and qualities. It simply means prioritizing the aspects that are most relevant and impactful to your clients' real estate journey. By focusing on their needs and aspirations, you create an environment where they feel supported, understood, and confident in their decision to work with you.

Recognize that certain aspects of your personal life may intersect with your business interactions. Be mindful about what you share on social media, especially when working with clients who are experiencing high levels of stress. Reinforce the notion that their real estate investment remains your top priority.

Strike a balance between your personal and professional life. While certain personal aspects may naturally surface in your business interactions, emphasize your expertise and commitment to your clients' success. By projecting a focused and knowledgeable image, you will establish trust, credibility, and a lasting impression as a trusted advisor in the real estate industry. It is through your actions and dedication to their best interests that clients will feel your genuine care and expertise.

I have observed that many agents fail to distinguish between their personal lives and their professional identity. This lack of differentiation hinders their ability to expand their network and restricts their potential for business growth.

I understand that transforming into someone you're not can be challenging and inauthentic; however, the objective is not to become someone entirely different, but rather to align your core values and purpose with your desired business identity. By evaluating and adjusting certain aspects of your behavior, communication, and presentation, you can shape your real estate personality and presentation in a way that resonates with your target audience and leaves a lasting impression.

Imagine yourself as the beautiful gift wrapping that adorns a carefully wrapped present. Think about the emotions that arise within you when you see a perfectly wrapped package with matching paper and a lovely bow. Consider the excitement and anticipation you feel when you receive a gift in a small blue box. These experiences evoke positive emotions and create a sense of value and appreciation. As a real estate professional, you want to elicit similar feelings in your clients through your visual presentation.

Just like the wrapping on a gift, your outer appearance and behavior should align with the core values you have established for yourself in Chapter Three. This does not mean pretending to be someone you are not, but rather presenting yourself in a way that reflects your professionalism and the values you hold dear. It is about being authentic and intentional in how you present yourself to the world.

By embodying the qualities and values that define your business, you become the visual representation of your brand. Your appearance, demeanor, and actions should all convey a sense of trustworthiness, expertise, and dedication. This is the "wrapping" that will attract clients and create a positive perception of your services.

Just as carefully chosen wrapping enhances the value of a gift, your attention to detail and commitment to excellence will enhance the perceived value of your real estate services. Clients will be drawn to your polished and professional image, which signals that you take your role seriously and are committed to providing an exceptional experience.

Think of your visual presentation as an extension of your brand. Consider the colors, styles, and overall aesthetic that align with your business identity. This includes everything from your attire to your marketing materials and online presence. Each element should be deliberately chosen to create a cohesive and appealing image that resonates with your target audience.

Creating a professional persona does not mean you have to present an image of being polished or driving a luxury vehicle to attract clients. The key is to align your image with the community and audience you are targeting.

If you are deeply rooted in a community that has a background in industries like oil or gas mining, or if your community is predominantly a military stopover, you will need to be relatable and authentic in your professional persona. For example, if your target audience is comprised of individuals transitioning from overseas and seeking permanent housing, you may find that a more casual, yet professional image resonates best with them.

In these scenarios, your attire may lean toward jeans paired with a blazer and comfortable shoes, which can create a sense of approachability and relatability. The goal is to present yourself in a way that appeals to the specific audience you are attracting, while still staying true to your values and maintaining a level of trustworthiness.

Ultimately, the most important aspect of your professional persona is to establish a connection with your audience. This connection is built on trust, understanding, and the ability to provide guidance and support during their important financial decisions. By presenting yourself in a way that resonates with your target audience, you create an environment where they feel comfortable and confident in working with you.

The key is to understand your community and audience, and then tailor your professional persona accordingly. By aligning your image with the values and expectations of your target market, you establish a strong foundation for building trust and fostering meaningful connections with your clients.

While the external appearance is important, you must also ensure that your behavior and actions align with the values you have established. Treat each client interaction as an opportunity to demonstrate your expertise, reliability, and dedication. By delivering on your promises and providing exceptional service, you reinforce the positive perception clients have of you.

The goal is to create an experience that evokes positive emotions and a sense of value in your clients. Just as a beautifully wrapped gift enhances the joy of receiving, your professional presentation enhances the perception of your services. By aligning your outer appearance and behaviors with your core values, you will create a powerful and memorable impression that sets you apart from the competition.

Think of yourself as the gift wrapping that represents your business. Consider the emotions and perceptions you want to evoke in your clients. By aligning your visual presentation with your core values and delivering exceptional service, you create a compelling and irresistible package that attracts clients and leaves a lasting impression.

As you embark on this process, maintain a clear connection with your why and your values. By staying true to your underlying motivations and beliefs, you ensure that the changes you make are aligned with your authentic self. This exercise involves auditing yourself and consciously shifting those elements of your personality that align with your envisioned business version.

This real estate personality you develop is the persona through which you will transact business. It is the embodiment of how you want people to perceive you and the experience you aim to create for them.

If you are unwilling to make changes in how the public perceives you in order to build your business, you risk limiting your potential buyer and seller audience. Each day that you choose not to shape your real estate personality, you not only lose one client, but also the potential clients they could have referred to you. This ripple effect can significantly impact the growth and success of your business.

Take a moment to reflect on the mathematics of this situation. By intentionally crafting your business persona and prioritizing the perceptions and experiences of your clients, you expand your reach and potential client base. Embracing this mindset allows you to unlock new opportunities and establish a strong foundation for ongoing success in the real estate industry.

An important aspect of marketing yourself effectively is to establish boundaries between your personal and professional platforms. By doing so, you can be intentional in reaching the specific individuals you envision as your target clients. This separation allows you to curate a professional image and connect with your intended audience more effectively.

Limiting what people see of your personal life is important because that curtain enables you to control the narrative and present yourself in a manner that aligns with your business goals. Consider the content you share on your public platforms and ensure it reflects the professional image you want to project. This includes being mindful of the photos, posts, and comments that you share, as they contribute to how people perceive you as a real estate professional.

By separating your personal and professional platforms, you can strategically tailor your messaging and content to appeal to your target clients. Your professional platforms, such as your business website, social media accounts, and professional networking profiles, should be designed to showcase your expertise, market knowledge, and value proposition. This focused approach ensures that your message reaches the right audience and aligns with their interests and needs.

Effective marketing is about creating a consistent and compelling brand presence. By intentionally separating your personal and professional platforms and aligning your messaging and content with your target audience, you attract and engage the individuals you envision as your ideal clients. This strategic approach sets the stage for building meaningful connections and ultimately growing your real estate business.

Consider developing a personal dress code that reflects your desired professional image and the values you want to convey to your clients. This dress code should align with your values and the type of clientele you aim to attract. Your dress code should serve as a walking biography that provides transparency of who you are and what you do. When you show up in the world as someone who does not align with their values, this creates doubt amongst the people you meet and will not attract clients. If you present yourself physically one way, but your message presents another version of you, you lose the ability to attract the people who will authentically and professionally be attracted to you.

I have dedicated a lot of time and effort evaluating my professional persona. I have carefully aligned my branding to create a unique combination of femininity and strength. The content I release is curated based on what is current and trending, while always staying true to the brand I have developed and the values I have chosen to live by. Additionally, I have implemented a dress code for myself to ensure that every interaction reflects a professional brand that exudes knowledge, competence, and a commitment to providing full-service support.

As I guide you in building your own brand, I will focus on the framework and content components in the next chapter. Before diving into that, I want you to step outside yourself and imagine you are a potential client looking in from the outside. For instance, imagine you work hard to maintain a fit physique and enjoy an active social life with Friday cocktails, Saturday beach days, and lazy Sunday afternoons. Over-sharing personal aspects of your life can be problematic, especially when it comes to your professional image. When envisioning your ideal client, consider whether they would be concerned with your appearance in a bathing suit or your opinion of the best place for a wine Wednesday. Keep in mind that people are often stressed about their real estate investments and want assurance that the person they are working with has their best interests at heart.

Think about whether a person going through a difficult divorce would want to work with someone they perceive as a potential threat or love interest to their soon-to-be ex-spouse. Similarly, consider if an 80-year-old woman, saddened by leaving her family home after four decades, would care about where you spent your Wednesday night getting the best cocktail deals. It is unlikely that a client looking to expand their rental portfolio would be interested in your vacation adventures with friends. In all these scenarios, the answer is clear:

personal aspects unrelated to the transaction and client's needs hold little relevance in the real estate business.

When I started in the industry, social media and the internet were not as prevalent as they are today, so I did not have a large audience with preconceived perceptions of me beyond my family, friends, and colleagues. I knew that I wanted to be relatable and believed that by showing up as my authentic self, I would attract like-minded individuals who saw the value in what I had to offer. I leaned into my corporate background, extensive experience in home renovations, and the juggling act of balancing work, parenthood, and life. People could relate to those aspects, and it resonated with them.

By focusing on being relatable and offering value through knowledge and stress reduction for my clients, I built meaningful connections and established a strong reputation in the industry. In real estate, the transaction is centered around providing knowledge and protecting clients from unnecessary stress. Emphasizing these aspects will enable you to attract clients who appreciate your expertise and the level of care you bring to their real estate journey.

I can appreciate that it is difficult to imagine yourself meeting people, nevertheless meeting them where they are at. I know of a lot of introverted real estate agents who do very well in the industry. Start by equipping yourself with knowledge and expanding into the audiences you already have (e.g., at a hair salon, the bank, or the grocery store). Real estate is a lifestyle as well as a career and whether you are introverted or not, this is a reality you have to come to terms with.

Many people are surprised when they find out I'm an introvert. I hate showing up late for things because everyone looks to see who didn't read the invitation and clearly didn't know when the party started. Find comfort in knowing that your vibe will be your tribe.

I created several small group environments where I could mingle and remind people that my business was in real estate. Rather than dishing out the traditional "buy a house from me/

sell a house with me", the topic of my renovations was a platform I could comfortably talk about without seeming salesy.

A lot of ways to market yourself do not include door knocking or networking in social settings. You must create environments you can comfortably network in. This might look like a small women's group that gets together to discuss the latest clothing or makeup trends, or it might be that you regularly put out information regarding the market or specifically properties in a social media platform. The key is to create engagement and invite others to interact with you.

Remember, your vibe will attract your tribe. By being open, genuine, and creating opportunities for engagement, you can effectively connect with potential clients who resonate with your approach. Do not be afraid to leverage your strengths as an introvert. Find unique ways to network and market yourself. With consistent effort and a focus on building meaningful connections, you can thrive in the real estate industry.

Adapt your approach to different social media platforms and meeting people where they are. Each platform attracts a different demographic and requires a tailored strategy to effectively engage with your audience. For example, LinkedIn is a professional networking platform where individuals seek business-related information. When using LinkedIn, present yourself as if you are attending a professional mixer or job interview. Share industry insights, market trends, and information that adds value to the business community. Keep your *LinkedIn* presence strictly focused on business. By adapting your approach to different platforms, maintaining consistency, and focusing on professionalism, you can effectively leverage social media and public platforms to connect with your audience and grow your real estate business. Aim to meet people's professional needs.

On the other hand, *Instagram* is a visual platform that appeals to a different demographic. Your *Instagram* content should align with your professional persona, but with a more personal touch. Share glimpses of your daily life within the boundaries of professionalism and your values. Focus on visually engaging content such as room decor ideas or video tours of properties. Encourage engagement and interaction by creating a visually appealing and relatable feed.

Facebook, like Instagram, is a visual platform but tends to attract an older audience. Although the content may be similar to *Instagram*, keep in mind the preferences and interests of this demographic. Older individuals are also potential buyers and sellers, so adapt your approach to resonate with their needs and preferences.

Consistency and alignment between your real estate persona and the public are key in social media marketing; however, you must recognize the unique nature of each platform and show up appropriately for each one. Just as you wouldn't wear a ball gown to a beach party, or stiletto heels to run a marathon, tailor your content and presentation to suit the platform and its audience.

While social media marketing tools like *Hootsuite* may offer convenience in sharing content across multiple platforms simultaneously, be cautious about maintaining the integrity of your message on each platform. Ensure that your content is customized for each platform to provide a seamless and engaging experience for your audience.

When using public platforms like your website, a blog, or social media, keep personal opinions to yourself. As a professional in the real estate industry, focus on providing valuable information, expertise, and insights related to your field. This helps maintain a professional image and avoids potential conflicts or controversies that may arise from personal opinions.

In the midst of the COVID-19 pandemic, the world witnessed countless debates and disagreements on various topics such as vaccinations and mask-wearing. These discussions often became heated and polarized with most people firmly entrenched in their own beliefs. Amidst these differing opinions, one thing remained constant—the real estate market continued to thrive, with buyers and sellers from various walks of life participating in transactions.

Real estate professionals must recognize that everyone is entitled to their own opinions and beliefs. When it comes to building your business, remain neutral and avoid openly expressing personal opinions that could potentially alienate clients or customers. In the early stages of your career, create an inclusive and welcoming environment for all individuals, regardless of their views or circumstances.

We all have our own opinions and biases. Personally, I have strong opinions about many subjects; however, I am mindful not to share them publicly or use my professional platforms to push personal agendas. By maintaining a neutral stance and refraining from openly expressing my opinions, I create an environment where potential clients feel comfortable reaching out to me, regardless of their own beliefs or life situations.

Kindness and empathy should be at the forefront of our interactions with others. We never truly know what someone else is going through, and by approaching everyone with compassion, we create a safe space where they feel heard and valued. After all, as a real estate professional, you are only a part of someone's journey, not their entire life journey. By aligning your public actions with your inner intentions and demonstrating how your expertise adds value to their journey, you will attract more clients and establish long-lasting relationships.

In the words of Paulo Coelho, "The world is changed by your example, not your opinion." This quote resonates deeply within the realm of real estate. It reminds us that actions speak louder than words, and that our behavior and professionalism have a far greater impact on others than our personal beliefs. By setting a positive example through your actions, professionalism, and commitment to serving your clients' needs, you inspire trust and confidence in those around you.

Maintaining neutrality and professionalism in your public interactions is key to attracting a wide range of clients and fostering meaningful connections. By refraining from sharing personal opinions and focusing on providing exceptional service, you will create an inclusive environment where clients feel comfortable seeking your guidance. Your example and actions have the power to shape the world around you and make a lasting impact on the lives of those you serve. As quoted by legendary investor Warren Buffet, "It takes twenty years to build a reputation and five minutes to ruin it. If you think about that, you'll do things differently."

CHAPTER FIVE
Who is Your Real Estate Personality?

*"By embodying the qualities and values
that define your business, you become the
visual representation of your brand."*
—**Marcia Bergen**

CHAPTER SUMMARY

In this chapter, I delved into the concept of a real estate personality, which sets a clear, intentional perception of who you want to be and is underpinned by your core values and business goals. Redefining your persona involves maintaining a balance between authenticity and professionalism, demonstrating empathy and understanding, and providing support tailored to each client's unique situation. I explored the role of cultivating a distinct professional persona in the real estate industry. This includes creating clear boundaries between personal and professional platforms, carefully tailoring content to align with the professional image you desire to project, and understanding your target audience to engage and resonate with them across different social media platforms. I underscored the importance of neutrality and refraining from expressing personal opinions that could alienate clients. All of this serves to wrap your business in a professional persona that conveys trustworthiness, expertise, and dedication to attract the clientele you desire and foster meaningful connections. Ultimately, your actions and the example you set have the power to shape your success in the real estate business.

REFLECTION QUESTIONS

1. In what ways can you build your network without directly selling yourself as a realtor? What else could you talk about?

2. How confident are you with your current social media skills? What could you confidently do today to promote yourself on social media? What do you need to learn?

3. Evaluate your social media platforms. Review your photos, posts, and comments to determine how others might perceive you.

4. Why is it important to maintain a neutral stance on topical issues, regardless of your own beliefs or life situation?

SCENARIOS

Scenario 1: You are meeting a prospective client who has recently been promoted to CEO of a prominent marketing company and is looking for an upgrade. She is in her mid-40s and lives alone with her dog. Considering what you have learned from this chapter, how would you dress and present yourself when meeting with this client?

Scenario 2: Someone in your social media network tagged you in an inappropriate photo of yourself, and it showed up on your professional *Facebook* page hours before you noticed—and the comments are rolling in! What do you do to regain your professionalism? What will you do in the future to mitigate similar incidents?

TO-DO LIST

- Define your real estate personality? What unique traits do you bring to the table that set you apart from the competition?

- Review your core values from Chapter 3. Do they represent your real estate personality? Make any adjustments necessary to ensure you are aligned.

- Develop a personal dress code that reflects your desired professional image and the values you want to convey to your clients.
- Review your social media accounts. Adjust privacy settings if you feel they do not align with your professional persona.
- Develop a content strategy for each platform that aligns with your professional image and caters to the unique demographics of each platform. You might choose to outsource this to a branded content specialist at some point, but I've provided a simple guide below to help you get started.

BUILDING A CONTENT STRATEGY: A BEGINNER'S GUIDE

Define Your Brand Identity: Begin by understanding your core values and the professional persona you aim to portray. Ensure that this aligns with your business goals and is separate from your private life.

Know Your Target Audience: Identify the needs, preferences, and demographics of your potential clients. Your content should be created to resonate with this group to reflect their interests and concerns.

Plan Your Content: Decide on content that will best convey your brand values and effectively engage your target audience. Your content could include blog posts, social media updates, videos, podcasts, webinars, or any other form that suits your business and audience.

Create Boundaries Between Personal and Professional Content: Ensure that your professional content remains separate from your personal content. Avoid overly personal or controversial topics that could alienate potential clients.

Platform-Specific Strategy: Customize your content strategy to suit the specific requirements of each social media platform you use. Different platforms cater to different demographics and require varying approaches for effective engagement.

Create a Content Calendar: Organize your content in advance and schedule it at regular intervals to maintain consistency and keep your audience engaged.

Audit and Adjust: Regularly monitor the efficacy of your content strategy and make necessary alterations. Utilize analytics tools to comprehend which content pieces are performing well, and why, and then modify your strategy in accordance with these insights.

Visual Branding: Select a color scheme that compliments your persona and utilize these colors as your brand palette. Make certain all visual elements in your content (including photos, graphics, colors, and fonts) are in sync with your brand identity and convey a sense of professionalism and reliability.

STEP-BY-STEP INSTRUCTIONS

- Read the chapter and highlight aspects you would like to reflect on further.
- Reflect on the questions provided and write down your responses.
- Complete the to-do list.
- Learn how to build a content strategy.
- Review your goals. Are you still on track?
- Review your real estate personality and personal dress code. Does it align with your goals?

TIPS AND TAKEAWAYS

- Maintain a professional yet authentic persona that resonates with your target clients.
- Work on establishing a connection with your audience built on trust and understanding.
- Align your behaviors and actions with your core values.
- Audit and align your social media with your envisioned business persona.
- Stick to business-related discussions on your professional platforms to maintain professionalism.
- Be mindful of the unique demographics of each social media platform.
- Keep a neutral stance on divisive issues to create an inclusive environment for all clients.

Your own takeaways:

- _____
  _____
- _____
  _____
- _____
  _____

CHAPTER SIX
Building Your Brand to Build Your Growth

". . . People will forget what you said,
people will forget what you did, but people
will never forget how you made them feel."
—Maya Angelou

I regularly visit a boutique wine store at a local Italian market. Another market is located just around the corner from my house, which is much more convenient for me to buy specialty food or wine. Both establishments have distinct inventories and offer a delightful range of ready-to-eat dishes, baked goods, fresh meat, and an impressive selection of wines. Despite the greater convenience of the closer market, I typically choose to go out of my way and shop at the less convenient one. This preference is based on a single factor: the exceptional level of service.

Upon entering the store, I receive a personalized greeting and almost always a recommendation for something new to try. The staff members are attentive to my preferences and remember my taste preferences. Furthermore, after I complete my purchases, one of the staff members consistently offers to assist me in taking my order to my vehicle. While I cannot definitively say which establishment has higher-priced food and wine, I believe they are competitive given the small size of the city I reside in and the mere ten-minute drive between the two markets. The remarkable level of service at the farther market makes any potential price difference well worth the longer drive.

Any business that aspires to gain customers' trust and loyalty must establish a strong foundation by first answering the fundamental question: what makes your business worthy of someone's time, money, and effort? When the transaction is complete, what will leave a lasting impression on your clients? To ensure sustained success, develop a foundation that can serve as a platform for growth and expansion.

First and foremost, the value you bring to your customers is paramount. You must offer a product or service that meets their needs and exceeds their expectations. This could be through high-quality craftsmanship, innovative solutions, or exceptional attention to detail. Whatever it may be, your offering must deliver value.

Moreover, customer experience plays a pivotal role in building a strong foundation. From the initial interaction to the post-purchase support, every touchpoint should leave a positive impression. Showcasing excellent communication, responsiveness, and genuine care for your customers' satisfaction will set you apart from the competition.

Building trust is another vital aspect. Honesty, transparency, and reliability are key in fostering trust with your clients. By delivering on promises, honoring commitments, and being accountable for any shortcomings, you establish credibility that resonates with your customers.

Furthermore, cultivating a strong brand identity is crucial for long-term success. Your brand should convey a clear message, values, and unique attributes that differentiate you from others in the market. Consistency in branding across all channels, coupled with a memorable visual identity, will help your clients remember and recognize you.

Ultimately, what will make clients remember you most is the overall experience you provide. It is the amalgamation of exceptional products or services, outstanding customer support, trustworthiness, and a well-defined brand that will leave a lasting impression.

By focusing on these foundational elements, you establish a strong base upon which to build and grow your business. Continually refining and enhancing these aspects will enable you to achieve sustained success and earn the loyalty and admiration of your clients.

To identify your target audience and shape your brand message, you must first understand your unique qualities and strengths. This message serves as your personal mission statement by encapsulating the purpose and essence of your brand. It reflects your aspirations and values while driving your actions and decisions, but as you grow and evolve personally, your mission statement may also undergo changes. As you gain new insights and experiences, your perspective on your brand's purpose and direction may shift. Embrace this evolution and allow your mission statement to adapt.

As your mission statement evolves, so should your brand. Your business should not be bound by limitations that hinder your progress. Continuously assess and reassess your brand to ensure it remains in harmony with your evolving vision. This may involve redefining your target audience, refining your brand message, or even exploring new avenues for growth.

Consistency between your brand and the service you deliver is vital at every stage of your business. Your brand promise should align with the actual experience your customers have. It is through delivering on your brand's promises that you build trust, loyalty, and a positive reputation.

Regularly evaluate the alignment between your brand and the service you provide. Seek feedback from your customers and take their input into account. Make necessary adjustments to bridge any gaps and maintain a strong connection between your brand image and the actual customer experience.

Your brand is not static. It is an organic entity that evolves alongside you. Embrace change, ensure coherence between your evolving mission statement and brand, and deliver a service that lives up to your brand's promises. By doing so, you will forge a strong and authentic connection with your audience and pave the way to long-term success.

In the realm of real estate branding, perception holds immense significance. It becomes your brand's reality. While you may invest considerable effort in crafting professionally designed social media posts, print materials, and scripted content, failing to live up to the brand you have meticulously built creates doubt in people's minds.

In today's digital age, approximately 90 percent of buyers and sellers will have explored your online presence before engaging with you. If their experience with you or the service you provide does not align with the image you have projected, it will undermine your potential for generating referrals and securing clients.

Once you have identified and defined your real estate persona, embody that identity in everything you do and everywhere you go within the realm of your business. Your brand should permeate every aspect of your professional life.

Your actions, demeanor, and service delivery must reflect the persona you have established. Align your personal interactions, conduct, and expertise with the brand image you wish to convey. By doing so, you solidify your brand's reputation and build trust with your clients and potential customers.

Your real estate persona should be evident in your marketing materials and in your daily interactions, networking events, and client engagements. Portray your brand identity across all touchpoints to strengthen your brand's authenticity and increase the likelihood of attracting loyal clients and generating valuable referrals.

By upholding your brand identity in every facet of your business, you establish a strong and reliable reputation. This, in turn, enhances your chances of success and allows you to maximize your business potential within the real estate industry.

Although I didn't grow up in the city I live in now, I have achieved success in listing properties and working with buyers in the mid to higher price points. The reason behind this success is simple: I built a brand that prioritizes elevating the client experience and placing their needs first. By carefully observing and evaluating my competition, I audited every aspect of their business and used that knowledge to offer additional services and build trust.

To build my brand, initially, I had a very feminine style and color palette, which naturally attracted mostly female clients. My brand also showcased my ability to explain home structures, clarify legal responsibilities, and foster community involvement. After recognizing the need to appeal to a broader audience, I made a deliberate choice to redefine and market myself as a progressive woman with a focus on presenting a conservative and professional image. This strategy aimed to make wives feel comfortable and husbands feel confident in working with me.

I took proactive steps to enhance my brand's visibility and credibility. First, I strategically managed my social media presence, and then I created videos and visual content that featured me renovating and preparing clients' homes. I also showcased before-and-after shots of home preparation efforts to let potential clients witness my expertise and dedication firsthand. This content became an integral part of my marketing efforts.

By carefully curating my brand's image and delivering exceptional service, I have succeeded in attracting clients in the mid to higher price points. My brand's transformation has since established me as a trusted and reputable professional in the industry.

Build a brand that reflects your current position and aligns with your future aspirations. Find balance in your ideal clientele. Focusing solely on promoting luxury properties or catering to high-end clients may limit your potential buyers to those seeking their first properties. Find a middle ground that encompasses both entry-level properties and your desired trajectory.

If you have defined yourself as someone who goes the extra mile for clients, have a clear understanding of what that entails. Defining your "extra mile" or value proposition will guide you in building a brand that aligns with the exceptional service you intend to provide. Let your actions be true to your words, as any disparity can erode trust and credibility, which can hinder the growth of your business.

Suppose you position yourself as a luxury realtor but always show up to showings or feature photos on your media platforms wearing torn jeans and a T-shirt. In that case, you risk alienating both luxury buyers and more laid-back clients. The luxury buyer may not believe in your ability to represent their high-end interests, while the casual client may not connect with your presentation. This inconsistency can lead to significant challenges in attracting and retaining clients.

To overcome this problem, align your brand image with the target audience and the services you provide. If your goal is to serve luxury clients, your brand should exude professionalism, sophistication, and attention to detail. Dressing appropriately for each occasion and presenting yourself in a manner that resonates with the luxury market will enhance your credibility and appeal to potential clients seeking high-end properties.

Similarly, if your target audience includes more relaxed and laid-back clients, your brand should reflect a sense of approachability, warmth, and authenticity. Tailoring your appearance and brand message to suit their preferences will help establish trust and create a connection with these clients.

Your brand is a representation of who you are and the service you offer. It should communicate your expertise, values, and dedication to clients. By building a brand that aligns with your intended audience and maintaining consistency in your actions, appearance, and messaging, you will establish a strong foundation for success in the industry.

One important aspect of your brand is having a clear and concise logo that incorporates your name to make it easily identifiable. To enhance brand recognition, select four to six colors for your social media posts and use them consistently or in combination. This approach will elevate your brand's visual identity and make it more recognizable to your audience.

In addition to a logo and visual elements, your brand should include a short mission statement that encapsulates your why. For instance, my mission statement is straightforward: Redefining your real estate experience.

This statement delivers the message that clients can expect something unique and different when working with me. Combining this messaging with a carefully thought-out visual image across all marketing materials (business cards, letters, calendars, and online platforms) is what makes me memorable.

To differentiate myself in the marketplace, I chose to create an Instagram layout using Canva that emulates the style of an account created by a fashion designer. This decision allowed me to stand out as unique and polished, setting myself apart from competitors. Your brand should reflect your desired image and convey a sense of professionalism and quality.

Branding evolves over time. My brand, for example, has transformed significantly from its early years in the business. Initially, I focused on marketing my hands-on approach to preparing homes for sale and self-staging. This emphasis was instrumental in gaining trust from sellers and demonstrating my expertise to buyers. As my business evolved over the past ten years, I stopped personally staging homes and doing the painting myself. I continue to offer these services and market my brand as customizable to include a range of services that are "included" in the commission.

By adapting your brand over time and aligning it with the changing needs and services you provide, you maintain a strong and relevant presence in the real estate market. Continuously refining and evolving your branding strategy allows you to effectively communicate the value you offer and ultimately leads to continued success and a memorable brand presence.

Branding yourself and creating a professional persona when starting a business is important, even if your primary goal is to generate income through activities like door knocking and calling expired listings. Building your brand helps people remember you and demonstrates your organization and knowledge.

When you share relevant and memorable content with consumers, they are more likely to remember you. Think about the brand Dove. Dove stands for embracing women as they are and promoting inclusivity. This recognition is a result of consistent messaging in all their marketing and advertising efforts. Dove has successfully built a brand that resonates with women and addresses their feelings of being unseen or undervalued, and making them believe that all women are valuable and loved.

When you overlook the value of building a professional or marketing profile that caters to potential buyers or sellers, you rely solely on the limited circle of family and friends to spread the word about your business. This significantly restricts your sphere of influence. Without providing compelling content and reasons why they should work with you, even your closest peers and family are unlikely to engage your services. Real estate is often the most significant asset for many people, and they want assurance that they are represented in a way that maximizes their investment. Failing to establish a strong brand and professional presence can be the difference between success and failure for many clients.

By investing time and effort into building your brand and creating a professional persona, you expand your reach, gain credibility, and inspire trust in potential clients. Through consistent messaging, quality content, and a clear value proposition, you position yourself as an expert in your field and build a reputation that attracts clients who value your expertise and trust you with their real estate needs. Your brand is a powerful tool that sets you apart from the competition and instills confidence in clients, which ultimately contributes to your success in the industry.

In today's digital age, a wealth of information is readily available at your fingertips. If you are unsure where to begin gathering relevant information, start with your local real estate board. Get to know the market trends specific to your city and each neighborhood. Many cities, including the one I reside in, have micro markets within the overall market. These micro markets can experience sudden shifts in inventory that can lead to significant changes in property values. Gain a clear understanding of market performance in different areas by searching within your database and utilizing the information portal provided by your local board.

Equipping yourself with knowledge helps you to become an expert in your field. Once you possess expertise, you can confidently share that knowledge with others. Consistency in branding and knowledge is a powerful tool. When you provide valuable insights and information, people will turn to you as a reliable source. This alignment between your branding and knowledge empowers potential clients to form a clear image and understanding of the value you offer.

By establishing yourself as a knowledgeable expert in your local market, you build credibility and trust with clients. People will seek out your expertise and rely on you to guide them through their real estate endeavors.

I have observed a concerning trend where both new and experienced real estate agents attempt to shortcut their branding and messaging by copying the branding of other agents or businesses. This approach carries two significant drawbacks. First, it lacks authenticity, which is needed to attract your target audience. Second, they inadvertently reinforce the brand being copied rather than differentiating themselves from competitors. As a result, not only does this strategy confuse potential clients about why they should choose to work with you, but it also drives them toward the original agent and brand that was copied.

Authenticity is a key element in building a successful brand. When you attempt to replicate someone else's branding, you miss the opportunity to showcase your unique qualities and value proposition. Each agent has their own strengths, expertise, and personal brand story. By imitating someone else's brand, you fail to communicate these distinctive attributes to your target audience, which makes it challenging for them to connect with you on a genuine level.

The primary objective of branding is to differentiate yourself from competitors and clearly communicate your unique value proposition. Develop a brand that accurately reflects who you are, what you offer, and the benefits clients can expect when working with you. By investing the time and effort into creating an authentic and distinctive brand, you attract the right audience—those who resonate with your message, values, and expertise.

Rather than seeking shortcuts or copying others, focus on developing a brand that highlights your individuality and expertise. Showcase your unique selling points and the specific benefits you bring to your clients. By doing so, you establish yourself as a trustworthy and credible agent and forge meaningful connections with your target audience.

Building a successful brand requires authenticity, differentiation, and a clear understanding of your unique value proposition. By avoiding the temptation to copy others, you cultivate a brand that attracts your ideal clients and sets you apart in a competitive market.

Auditing your brand on an annual basis, rather than completely reinventing it, is a wise practice that ensures you continue to build upon the foundation you already established. Rebuilding your brand from scratch requires starting over and risking the loss of the audience you have diligently cultivated.

As part of my routine, I dedicate numerous hours each December and January, when the market is typically slower, to review my marketing materials and assess how I can improve them. I refrain from reinventing my logo or website and instead focus on enhancing the material and messaging to reflect the growth and lessons I gained over the previous year.

For instance, I developed a PowerPoint listing presentation that incorporates the new services I added to my business. I created buyer and seller guides that align more cohesively with my website. I elevated the approach to conducting open houses by implementing a clear plan that my team and I follow at every open house. This strategic planning attracts potential sellers who attend our open houses, as it provides them with a glimpse of the level of branding and service I offer.

To leave a lasting impression, I have implemented various branded items and enhancements during open houses. For example, I provide branded water bottles and distribute small bags of popcorn with labels that read "Thanks for popping by." Additionally, I display a neighborhood map on a pinboard that highlights the locations of schools, community centers, shopping centers, and other amenities in relation to the subject property. I also include my top five dining or entertainment recommendations. Branded welcome mats at the entrance further reinforce my brand identity. Collectively, these elements strengthen my brand presence and create a memorable and elevated experience for potential clients.

By reinforcing my brand through these tangible and thoughtful touches, I leave a lasting impression on those who interact with my business. These efforts reinforce my brand identity and demonstrate the level of service and attention to detail I provide. This comprehensive approach helps me stand out from the competition and creates a positive and memorable impression in the minds of potential clients.

Auditing and refining your brand annually allows you to evolve and improve while maintaining the foundation you have already built. By enhancing your marketing materials and reinforcing your brand through memorable experiences, you establish a strong and lasting connection with your audience.

When I conduct a walk-through of someone's home to determine its value or assess potential renovations or improvements to increase its worth, I make sure to leave a branded thank-you card in the mailbox before I leave. Within a branded folder, I enclose either a buyer guide or seller guide, along with a branded calendar and comparable sales data specific to their neighborhood, based on their tax assessment. While these comparable sales serve as a loose target since I haven't yet explored the interior of the home, they demonstrate to my potential clients that I have a comprehensive understanding of their neighborhood and a clear vision and plan for their buying or selling experience. Utilizing every interaction as an opportunity to define myself and my brand is a principle I wholeheartedly embrace.

I firmly believe in the proverb "Live today the way you want to be remembered tomorrow," as coined by Dillon Burroughs. This philosophy underscores my approach to my real estate business. I strive to leave a lasting impression on everyone I interact with while upholding the values and vision of my brand. By doing so, I aim to be remembered as a trusted and dedicated professional who goes above and beyond for clients.

Leaving a branded thank-you card in the mailbox of the homes I evaluate serves multiple purposes. First, it demonstrates gratitude and appreciation for the homeowners' time and willingness to let me assess their property. This small gesture shows that I value their trust and view them as important individuals. Second, the buyer or seller guide I leave behind in a branded folder offers valuable information tailored to their specific needs. This educational resource showcases my expertise and commitment to guiding clients through their real estate journey. Additionally, the inclusion of a branded calendar serves as a practical item that reminds clients of my brand throughout the year.

The inclusion of comparable sales data within their neighborhood further solidifies my position as a knowledgeable and attentive real estate professional. Although these sales figures are based on assessments and not the interior inspection of their home, they provide an initial understanding of the market and a glimpse into the potential value of their property. By demonstrating my familiarity with their neighborhood and outlining a clear plan, I instill confidence in potential clients that I possess the expertise and vision to successfully navigate their real estate transactions.

Every interaction I have with people is an opportunity to define myself and my brand. Whether it is a walk-through, a client consultation, or a casual conversation, I strive to leave a positive and memorable impression. By delivering a high level of service, demonstrating professionalism, and showcasing my brand's values, I aim to build long-lasting relationships and foster a strong reputation within the industry.

Ultimately, I believe that the way I conduct myself today will shape how I am remembered tomorrow. Therefore, I remain committed to continuously refining and enhancing my brand. I take advantage of every opportunity to positively influence others' perception of me and leave a lasting impression that aligns with my brand's values and mission.

As your brand develops, be cautious about completely forsaking one brand in favor of another. This can be compared to renaming a well-established company, which may result in the loss of followers and clients who have become familiar with your existing brand.

CHAPTER SIX
Building Your Brand to Build Your Growth

*". . . People will forget what you said,
people will forget what you did, but people
will never forget how you made them feel."*
—**Maya Angelou**

CHAPTER SUMMARY

This chapter emphasized the role of branding and service quality in building a successful personal business identity. I discussed how to differentiate oneself from competing realtors, evolve your brand to broaden its appeal, and align your brand with your target audience, and how your actions must reflect your brand's promise. I advised you to engage in annual audits of your brand to ensure continuous improvement while maintaining your foundational identity. I emphasized how every interaction (or touchpoint) you have with a prospective client is an opportunity to reinforce your brand, and how the impressions you make today will shape how you will be remembered in the future. I also encouraged you to look up your local real estate board to start developing a deep understanding of market trends, micro markets, and market performance in different areas within your region.

REVIEW

Any business that aspires to gain customers' trust and loyalty must establish a strong foundation. Review these points from Chapter 6 to set up your business for growth and expansion:

The value you bring to your customers is paramount. Always strive to meet customers' needs and exceed their expectations.

The customer experience plays a pivotal role in building a strong foundation. Showcasing excellent communication, responsiveness, and genuine care for your customers' satisfaction will set you apart from the competition.

Building trust is vital. Honesty, transparency, consistency, accountability, and reliability show your clients that they can trust you.

Cultivate a strong brand identity. Your brand should have a visual identity that conveys a clear message that reflects your values and highlights the unique attributes that differentiate you from others in the market.

By focusing on these foundational elements, you establish a strong base upon which to build and grow your business.

REFLECTION QUESTIONS

1. Can you recall a time when you chose one business over another due to its exceptional service? How did that impact your perception of the brand?
2. What steps can you take to ensure consistency in your brand's visual identity across all marketing materials?
3. What unique qualities and value proposition can you bring to your target audience in the real estate market?
4. How are you currently demonstrating or building your expertise in the real estate market? Have you discovered any new tools in your journey?
5. In what ways can you differentiate your brand from competitors?

SCENARIOS

Scenario 1: Imagine you own a real estate business that primarily deals with luxury properties. Your brand has been well-established and is recognized for its high-end, professional image; however, you've recently noticed a market opportunity for mid-range properties in a thriving neighborhood. How would you approach this change while maintaining the integrity and perception of your brand?

Scenario 1: It's your first pitch to a prospective client as a newly minted real estate agent. You have to prepare a PowerPoint presentation that you hope will win them over. Given what you have learned in this chapter, what visual aspects of the presentation will you incorporate to communicate your professional brand persona?

TO-DO LIST

- If applicable, assess your current brand identity and list its strengths and weaknesses.
- Review the mission statement you wrote in Chapter 3. Does it continue to encapsulate your brand's purpose and identity?
- Create (or, if it's in your budget, have a designer create) a clear and concise logo that incorporates your name. Choose one complimentary font to go with the logo and use it consistently in all your communications.
- Choose four to six colors that you will use in your social media posts, website, branded items and materials, and stationary, etc.
- Make a list of branded items or materials you could create to distribute at open houses or client meetings. Research vendors and get quotes.
- Experiment with online design tools such as Canva to create branded posts, stationary, branded items and materials, cards, etc.

- Look up your local real estate board. Identify the market trends specific to your city and neighborhood. Try to identify any micro markets.

STEP-BY-STEP INSTRUCTIONS

1. Read the chapter and take notes.
2. Complete the reflection questions and scenarios and write down your responses.
3. Complete the to-do list.
4. Work out the visual identity of your brand, either with a designer or on your own, and experiment with branding your content and assets. Get feedback from trusted friends and colleagues. Launch once you are confident with your brand—trust me, you can rack up extra costs and confuse your audience if you keep changing your "look."
5. Review your goals from the previous chapters. Do they still align with your persona? Make adjustments, if necessary.

TIPS AND TAKEAWAYS

- Regular customer feedback is a powerful tool for understanding how well your brand promise aligns with the actual customer experience.
- Your brand is an evolving entity. Don't be afraid to let it grow and adapt with you.
- Create a visual brand that is timeless and/or can easily evolve with your business.
- Maintain consistency in your brand's visual identity across all platforms to enhance brand recognition.
- Regularly review and update your brand to ensure it remains relevant and appeals to your target audience.
- Use the slow market periods to review and improve your branding materials.
- Always leave potential clients with something branded that they can keep and use.

Your own takeaways:

- _____
  _____

- _____
  _____

- _____
  _____

CHAPTER SEVEN
Getting Out of Your Own Way

*"If you want something you
have never had, you must be willing to
do something you have never done."*
—Thomas Jefferson

During a recess break when I was eight years old, my best friend made a comment about my freckles, suggesting that they were the result of not washing my face. In a desperate attempt to make them disappear, I decided to vigorously scrub my nose with a cleaning sponge the day before our annual school photos. Needless to say, my efforts did not yield the desired outcome. Instead, I ended up with a large raw red spot resembling a small mandarin orange on the top and sides of my nose.

On Grade 3 picture day, I showed up to school with this conspicuous mark on my face, which eventually turned into a scab. For two weeks, I had to go to school with this visible reminder of my ill-fated attempt to get rid of my freckles. To my surprise, my teacher noticed and called me aside to inquire about what had happened. When I explained the situation, she gave me a warm hug and reassured me that freckles are not something that can be washed away.

This childhood experience taught me an important lesson about embracing and accepting who I am, freckles and all. It made me realize that trying to conform to society's standards of beauty or attempting to change aspects of myself to fit in is not only futile but also unnecessary. Each of us is unique, and our individual traits, including freckles, are part of what makes us special.

As you went through the process of dissolving the myths of the real estate industry, and then defining yourself and understanding who your ideal client will be, the next step is to recognize when you are getting in your own way. It is common to allow our past fears of failure or concern ourselves with what others think of us. To find true success and be seen, you must step aside and tear away your own roadblocks.

As I reflect on this memory, I draw parallels to the real estate industry. Just as I learned to embrace my freckles and accept myself for who I am, real estate professionals must embrace their authentic selves. In a world where appearances and perceptions matter, it can be tempting to conform to certain standards or project an image that aligns with societal expectations; however, the true key to success lies in being genuine and true to oneself.

Clients look for someone they can trust and relate to, and who understands their needs and can guide them through important decisions. By being authentic and showing up as our true selves, we create a foundation of trust and establish connections with our clients on a deeper level.

In the industry, our value as professionals is not solely determined by our appearance or the image we project, but the knowledge, expertise, and personalized service we provide. When we embrace our true selves, we attract clients who resonate with our authenticity and appreciate the unique value we bring to the table.

So, whether you have freckles, wear glasses, or have any other distinguishing features, embrace them as part of your personal brand. Your clients will appreciate your genuine approach, and you will be able to build stronger, more meaningful relationships based on trust and authenticity. It is not about conforming to societal standards, but about being the best version of yourself in this dynamic and rewarding industry.

Entering any business where your face will be prominently featured can be challenging when it comes to accepting our perceived flaws and projecting your mission to the world. It is natural to feel vulnerable and fearful about how others will perceive you and what they may say about you.

It is human nature to have insecurities and concerns about our appearance. We all have aspects of ourselves that we may not particularly like or feel self-conscious about, but these perceived flaws are part of what makes us unique and special. Our imperfections make us relatable, and relatability is what fosters connection with others.

When we allow ourselves to be vulnerable and show up authentically, it creates a genuine connection with our audience and potential clients. By acknowledging our own vulnerabilities, we create a space for others to do the same and make room for deeper and more meaningful connections.

The opinions and judgments of others are beyond your control. You cannot please everyone, and there will always be people who criticize or have something negative to say, but their opinions do not define you or determine your worth. What matters most is that you stay true to yourself and your mission and attract people who resonate with your authentic self.

When we embrace our vulnerabilities and overcome the fear of judgment, we give ourselves the freedom to fully express our mission and connect with others in a meaningful way. It is through this authenticity that we build trust and establish long-lasting relationships with clients who appreciate us for who we are.

Real estate agents surround themselves with a supportive network of individuals who uplift and encourage them. Seek out mentors, colleagues, or friends who can provide guidance, support, and reassurance as you navigate this industry. They help remind you of your worth and reinforce the importance of staying true to yourself.

No one is perfect. We all have our own insecurities. Embrace your vulnerabilities, accept yourself as you are, and focus on the value you bring to the table. Your unique qualities, combined with your knowledge, skills, and passion for your work, will be what sets you apart from the competition.

While it may be daunting to face the fear of judgment and vulnerability, embracing your true self and projecting your mission with authenticity builds genuine connections and improves the chance of succeeding in the industry. Acceptance of your perceived flaws and understanding that they are a part of what makes you unique will ultimately allow you to thrive and create meaningful relationships with clients who appreciate your genuine self. Embrace your vulnerabilities, surround yourself with support, and let your authentic self shine through.

I can relate to the challenges by reflecting on what I faced as a young mother in a small town with religious ties. It's unfortunate that societal norms and judgments often create a sense of shame and scrutiny for individuals who deviate from those norms. The pressure to conform and the fear of being judged can be overwhelming.

Becoming a mother at such a young age brought about a unique set of challenges and stigmas. It is disheartening that having premarital sex, a personal choice, led to feelings of guilt and being labeled a sinner by people who were raised or taught to deflect their own insecurities by judging others. The perception that others were constantly watching and waiting for me to fail added to the pressure and discomfort I experienced during that time.

Ultimately, the opinions of others did not define my worth, and they do not define your worth or determine your path to success. My journey as a young mother allowed me to discover two significant truths about myself. First, I realized that I have the strength and determination to overcome obstacles and achieve my goals when I put my heart and soul into something. Resilience and perseverance served me well as I navigated the challenges of entrepreneurship.

Second, I gained insight into the nature of human judgment. People often form opinions about others when they themselves are uncomfortable with their own identity or choices. Their opinions reflect their own insecurities and should not dictate how you perceive yourself or your potential for success.

Entering the world of business, regardless of the industry, can be uncomfortable and may make you feel like you're constantly under scrutiny. Stepping out of your comfort zone and taking risks is a necessary part of personal and professional growth. Embracing these challenges and learning from them will enable you to develop the skills and mindset needed to thrive in your field.

Surround yourself with a supportive network of individuals who believe in you and your capabilities. While there may be people who doubt or judge you, there are also those who will uplift and inspire you along the way. Seek out mentors, like-minded peers, and individuals who have overcome similar challenges. They can provide guidance, encouragement, and serve as a reminder that success is possible, regardless of the judgments and opinions of others.

The path to success is unique for everyone. Stay true to yourself and your values. Embrace your journey, including the challenges and experiences that shaped you and use them as sources of strength and motivation. As you grow as an entrepreneur, strive to create a supportive and inclusive environment that celebrates diversity and empowers others to pursue their dreams.

It can be difficult to face judgments and assumptions from others, so stay focused on your own path and believe in your abilities. Your past experiences, including the challenges you overcame, have equipped you with resilience and determination. Surround yourself with a supportive network and remember that your worth and potential for success are not defined by the opinions of others. Embrace the discomfort by stepping out of your comfort zone and continuing to grow and thrive as an entrepreneur.

Brené Brown's work on vulnerability has resonated with many people, myself included. The idea of showing up as our authentic selves without the armor of societal expectations or fear of judgment is both empowering and challenging. It requires us to dig deep, confront our insecurities, and redefine our relationships with others and ourselves.

When we talk about armor, it is not physical protection but rather the emotional barriers and masks we put on to shield ourselves from vulnerability. We often hide behind these facades to present a version of ourselves we believe will be more accepted or validated by others. When we do this, we lose touch with our true selves and fail to show up authentically.

Showing up authentically means being true to who we are, with all our strengths, weaknesses, and imperfections. It means embracing vulnerability and being willing to be seen for who we truly are, without pretenses or facades. This is not an easy task, as it requires us to let go of our fear of judgment and rejection.

Brené Brown emphasizes the importance of having the people whose opinions truly matter in our front row or cheerleading seats. These are the individuals who support us, believe in us, and accept us for who we are. When we have these people in our corner, their opinions hold weight and influence in our lives. These individuals must be distinguished from the larger audience whose opinions should not dictate our actions or define our worth.

Identifying whose opinions truly matter is a critical step in embracing vulnerability. When we are clear on our why and our values, we become less susceptible to the judgments of others. We focus on what truly matters and the actions we need to take to achieve our goals and build our business. Consistency becomes key, as we align our actions with our authentic selves, regardless of external opinions.

Vulnerability is a universal experience. We all feel it to some degree, and no one enjoys exposing themselves to potential judgment or criticism. Brené Brown encourages us to remember that if the individuals who pass judgment are not in our front row, their opinions should not hold power over us. We should prioritize the opinions and feedback of those who genuinely support and uplift us.

Overcoming the fear of vulnerability and embracing our authentic selves is an ongoing process. It requires self-reflection, self-acceptance, and courage. It's not about seeking external validation or conforming to societal expectations, but rather finding the strength to show up as our true selves, even when it feels uncomfortable or uncertain.

As we navigate the realm of business and entrepreneurship, vulnerability becomes even more crucial. Building authentic connections with clients and colleagues requires us to let go of the armor and create a space of trust and openness. By showing up authentically, we attract like-minded individuals who resonate with our values and mission. This authenticity fosters genuine connections, builds trust, and ultimately contributes to the growth and success of our business.

In conclusion, Brené Brown's insights on vulnerability challenge us to strip away the armor and show up as our authentic selves. The process requires self-reflection, courage, and the willingness to prioritize the opinions of those who truly matter. By embracing vulnerability, we create a foundation for meaningful connections and empower ourselves to build a business based on authenticity and integrity.

As you embark on your journey of personal growth and business development, understand that not everyone will be comfortable with your success and growth. Their discomfort is not a reflection of you, but rather a reflection of their own insecurities and limitations.

There will always be people who are uncomfortable in their own situations, and they may project their discontent onto you. They may struggle with feelings of envy, resentment, or inadequacy, which can manifest as criticism or judgment toward your achievements. This type of person is not your cheerleader, and their opinions should not hold power over your self-worth or hinder your progress.

Your cheerleaders are the people who truly know and love you. They are the ones who support and respect you unconditionally. They understand the challenges and sacrifices you make as you step outside your comfort zone and pursue your goals. Cheerleaders are not threatened by your success; instead, they celebrate your efforts and accomplishments. They provide the encouragement and praise that fuel your motivation and drive.

Surrounding yourself with positive influences, such as your cheerleaders, is instrumental in navigating the challenges of personal and professional growth. They uplift and inspire you, and provide the support and validation you need to stay focused on your journey. Their unwavering belief in you serves as a powerful reminder of your worth and potential. Their perspective is grounded in a deep understanding of your character and journey. Their encouragement and celebration of your wins are genuine and heartfelt, reinforcing your belief in yourself.

Stay true to your vision and purpose, even in the face of criticism or judgment from others. Embrace the power of your cheerleaders and lean on their unwavering support as you navigate the challenges and triumphs on your path.

The journey of building a successful business is not without its challenges and moments of self-doubt. The conflict between courage and fear can arise frequently, testing your resolve and commitment; however, you alleviate the grip of fear by embracing clarity on your why and value proposition, equipping yourself with knowledge and statistics, and presenting your authentic real estate persona.

Your business persona helps navigate the conflict between courage and self-doubt. By presenting yourself authentically, you build trust and credibility with your clients and peers.

Remain true to who you are while embracing the professional image and branding that aligns with your business goals. When your actions and words are congruent with your values and purpose, you establish a solid foundation for overcoming self-doubt and inspiring confidence in others.

Staying aligned with your why helps you maintain your motivation and keep your focus. Your why represents your deeper purpose and the driving force behind your business endeavors. It is the underlying reason why you chose to embark on this journey and make a difference in the lives of your clients. By continuously reminding yourself of your why, you tap into a reservoir of determination and passion that pushes you through moments of self-doubt.

As you commit to your pillars of business (to be discussed in the next chapter), embody your authentic business persona, and stay aligned with your why, you will redefine your comfort zone. What was once unfamiliar and intimidating will gradually become your new normal. Each step you take outside of your comfort zone becomes an opportunity for growth and development. Embracing these challenges and facing them with courage will strengthen your resilience and expand your capabilities.

Fear and self-doubt are natural responses to stepping into the unknown. Instead of allowing them to paralyze you, acknowledge their presence and use them as fuel for growth. Embrace the discomfort, knowing that on the other side lies personal and professional transformation. Recognize that courage is not the absence of fear, but rather the willingness to take action despite the presence of fear.

The conflict between courage and self-doubt is an ongoing battle that arises on the journey of building a successful business. By embracing clarity of your why, equipping yourself with knowledge, presenting your authentic real estate persona, and committing to your three pillars of business, you can navigate this conflict with resilience and determination. Fear may persist, but it does not have to define your actions or hinder your progress. Choose to step outside of your comfort zone, redefine it, and embrace the growth opportunities that lie ahead. With each courageous step, you inch closer to realizing your goals and making a meaningful impact in the world of real estate.

When I first entered the real estate business, platforms like *TikTok* and *Instagram* reels weren't even on the horizon. The thought of having to put myself out there, not just on signs or in print ads, but through creating meaningful content and sharing it with the world, was daunting. I couldn't help but let out a sigh of relief as I wrote this, realizing the immense pressure that comes with the ever-evolving media landscape.

In today's digital age, it is almost impossible to avoid the need to produce content and share your message in various formats. This can be both exciting and overwhelming. You may find yourself grappling with questions like, "What if my hair and makeup aren't perfect today?" or "Can't I just lose ten or twenty pounds before I attempt to create videos?"

Perfection is not a prerequisite for putting yourself out there. In fact, striving for perfection can often hinder your progress and hold you back from sharing your unique voice and perspective. The truth is, your audience is more interested in authenticity and relatability than flawless appearances.

Instead of focusing on your physical attributes, shift your mindset toward the value you provide and the impact you can make through your content. Your expertise, knowledge, and insights are what will resonate with your audience and attract potential clients. People want to connect with a real person who understands their needs and can guide them through the complexities of the real estate world.

Embrace the fact that you are a work in progress, just like everyone else. Emphasize your strengths, knowledge, and passion for real estate. You don't need to have all the answers or be the epitome of perfection. Your willingness to learn, grow, and share experiences is what will make you relatable and trustworthy.

If you're concerned about your appearance, remember that your audience is likely more forgiving and understanding than you give them credit for. Authenticity is far more captivating than an artificially polished image. Embrace your unique features, quirks, and imperfections. Let your personality shine through and focus on providing value to your audience.

As for the fear of being on camera, remember that practice makes perfect. Start small and then gradually push yourself outside your comfort zone. Experiment with different formats and styles of content. You will find your rhythm and confidence as you gain more experience.

As you experiment, cultivate a positive self-image and practice self-compassion. Realize that your worth extends far beyond your physical appearance. Embrace self-care practices that boost your confidence and nurture your well-being. You are more than enough, just as you are, and your value in the real estate industry is not determined by your physical attributes.

The need to produce content and share your message in today's digital landscape can be daunting, but it also presents exciting opportunities for connection and growth. Concerns about your appearance or fears of imperfection will only hold you back. Embrace authenticity, focus on the value you bring, and remember that your audience wants to connect with a real person, flaws and all. Practice self-compassion, cultivate a positive self-image, and gradually step out of your comfort zone. With time and experience, you will find your voice and create meaningful content that resonates with your audience.

One of the lessons I learned after growing my business quickly, and one that I've observed in other successful agents, is the importance of being seen. It requires a willingness to shed the facade and let go of the barriers that hold us back from showing up authentically for the people who need to see us. I understand that this can be a scary proposition, but I assure you that genuine visibility armed with knowledge and a carefully crafted presence will propel your business forward at an accelerated pace.

Embracing this concept was a significant challenge for me. The rapid advancements in technology left me with no alternative but to summon the courage to show up, despite the inherent risks of potential ridicule or negative comments. I quickly came to realize that there was no way around it if I wanted to stay relevant and effectively reach my target audience.

The most important piece of advice I would offer anyone just starting to build a business is to be crystal clear on your why. Understanding your purpose, driving motivation, and core values will serve as the guiding force behind your actions. It will anchor you when faced with doubts or difficulties and empower you to keep showing up, no matter how challenging it may seem at first.

Acknowledge that this discomfort and fear of judgment will gradually dissipate as you continue to show up and experience even the smallest victories along the way. Each achievement, no matter how seemingly insignificant, reinforces your confidence and validates the path you're on.

Building a business is not an overnight process. It requires consistency, perseverance, and a willingness to evolve. The initial discomfort you may feel will pale in comparison to the satisfaction and fulfillment that comes from making a positive impact and building meaningful relationships with your clients.

To overcome this hurdle, start by taking small steps outside your comfort zone. Begin by sharing your expertise and insights on platforms that align with your target audience's preferences, such as social media channels or industry-specific forums. Gradually expand your reach and experiment with different formats of content creation, such as videos, blog posts, or podcasts. Strike a balance between showcasing your professional knowledge and highlighting your authentic self. People are drawn to genuine connections, so be yourself while maintaining a professional demeanor that instills confidence and trust in your audience.

As you embark on this journey, keep in mind that setbacks and challenges are inevitable. Learn from them, adapt, and always stay true to your values and your purpose. Surround yourself with a support network of like-minded individuals who understand and appreciate the journey you're on. Seek guidance from mentors or peers who have successfully navigated similar paths and can offer insights and encouragement.

When embarking on a new business venture, it is common to face financial constraints, especially in the early stages, but you can leverage cost-effective methods to effectively communicate your message and reach your target audience. Two valuable avenues for achieving this are social media and in-person meetings, both of which offer great potential for growing your business without breaking the bank.

Social media platforms have emerged as powerful tools for marketing and branding, and offer a broad and targeted audience engagement. With various platforms available, such as *Facebook*, *Instagram*, *Twitter*, and *LinkedIn*, you can choose the ones that align best with your business and target market. Social media allows you to create and share content, engage with your audience, and build brand awareness—all at a minimal cost. By consistently delivering valuable and relevant content, you establish your expertise and attract potential clients.

When developing your social media and online presence, prioritize organic growth and engagement. While it may be tempting to purchase followers to create the illusion of being an influential figure, the true measure of success lies in genuine engagement. Without active engagement from real and interested individuals, your online platforms will not generate the desired results.

Focusing on local connections and building relationships with individuals directly related to your business establishes a network that can yield tangible business opportunities. Rather than seeking an abundance of followers from various locations with no direct connection to your industry or potential referrals, concentrate on cultivating meaningful connections with real people who have a genuine interest in your field.

Engaging with your local community, attending industry events, and actively participating in relevant groups or forums help establish your credibility and increase your visibility among potential clients and collaborators. By targeting individuals and organizations that align with your business goals, you can develop a network that is more likely to yield referrals and contribute to your success.

Boost engagement on your social media platforms by providing valuable content that resonates with your target audience. Sharing informative articles, industry insights, success stories, and tips related to your field attract and retain a loyal following. Encouraging interaction through thoughtful questions, polls, or calls to action can also stimulate engagement and create a sense of community.

Authenticity and genuine connections should be the foundation of your online presence. Building trust and establishing yourself as an industry expert with valuable content will attract an engaged audience that sees the value in your offerings. Social media success is not measured solely by the number of followers, but rather by the level of engagement, meaningful connections, and tangible business opportunities that arise from those platforms.

In addition to online platforms, in-person meetings provide an opportunity for building relationships and connecting with your target audience on a personal level. Networking events, industry conferences, and community gatherings offer avenues to meet potential clients and establish rapport. While attending such events may involve some expenses, they can provide a strong return on investment by creating meaningful connections and generating leads.

As you progress in your business, diversify your marketing and outreach strategies to maximize your reach and impact. In upcoming chapters, we will explore other cost-effective methods to deliver your message, such as content marketing, email campaigns, and partnerships. These strategies can help you expand your reach, increase brand visibility, and nurture relationships with potential clients.

Content marketing, for instance, involves creating and sharing valuable and informative content (blog posts, videos, or podcasts) that resonates with your target audience. By offering insights, tips, and resources, you establish yourself as a trusted authority in your field and attract interested prospects. Content marketing is highly flexible and can be tailored to fit your budget and resources, making it an effective and cost-efficient method to engage with your audience.

Email campaigns, on the other hand, allow you to stay connected with your existing network and nurture leads. By regularly sending out targeted and personalized emails, you can provide updates, share valuable content, and promote your services. Email marketing platforms offer affordable solutions to manage and automate your campaigns to ensure that your messages reach the right people at the right time.

Partnerships and collaborations are another cost-effective way to expand your reach and tap into new networks. By teaming up with complementary businesses or industry influencers, you can leverage their audience and expertise to gain exposure and attract potential clients. Joint events, cross-promotions, or guest appearances are just a few examples of how partnerships can amplify your reach and generate new leads.

When starting a business with limited capital, utilize cost-effective methods to deliver your message and reach your target audience. Social media platforms and in-person meetings offer great opportunities to engage with potential clients and build relationships. As your business grows, consider incorporating additional strategies such as content marketing, email campaigns, and partnerships to maximize your reach and impact. By being strategic and resourceful, you can effectively market your business while staying within your budget.

When entering the real estate market, be prepared for various types of conversations such as negotiating deals and managing conflicts. These are integral parts of the business, and developing the skills to navigate such conversations will greatly contribute to your success.

One common scenario involves discussing price reductions with sellers. Asking a seller for a price reduction can get uncomfortable, especially if you're new to the industry, but these conversations are necessary to market and sell properties. Instead of focusing on personal finances or making it a confrontational discussion, approach it from a data-driven perspective. Use market statistics, recent sales in the neighborhood, and the competition to explain the need for a price adjustment. By presenting this information objectively, you help sellers understand the market realities and make informed decisions.

From the beginning of the agent–client relationship, set clear expectations and establish a step-by-step marketing plan. When meeting with sellers, outline your approach, including regular updates on activity, feedback, and market conditions. Let them know that you will have price discussions after a specific time frame, such as twenty-one days on the market, to allow for sufficient exposure and data collection. Additionally, explain the importance of adjusting the price if the property is not generating sufficient interest or offers. By providing sellers with a clear roadmap and demonstrating your expertise in interpreting market trends, you establish trust and align expectations from the beginning.

If managing conflict or difficult conversations does not come naturally to you, scripting can be a valuable tool. Various scripting techniques and styles are available to help you navigate challenging discussions with confidence and professionalism. By practicing and internalizing scripted responses, you ensure that your communication remains clear and effective. Scripts provide a framework for addressing common objections, negotiating terms, or discussing sensitive topics that allow you to maintain control of the conversation and guide it toward a favorable outcome.

Managing conflict and engaging in necessary conversations is a skill that can be developed with practice and experience. Over time, as you gain more confidence and refine your communication strategies, these conversations will become easier to handle. Embrace the opportunity to learn and grow from each interaction, continuously improving your ability to manage conflicts and negotiate effectively.

One of the ways we often sabotage ourselves is by constantly worrying about what others think of us. We become concerned about the opinions and judgments of those around us, and this fear can hinder our progress and success.

Reflecting on my own experience in high school, when I became pregnant during my teenage years, I faced a significant challenge. In a small town with its own set of moral values, it was deemed unacceptable for a pregnant student to continue attending a public high school. I vividly remember being called into the principal's office, where I was asked to confirm my pregnancy and then told to stop attending classes immediately. It was a difficult and emotional moment for me, but I made a conscious decision that my education was my own choice, not someone else's. With the support of my parents, I returned to school the following day and continued my studies as usual, despite the whispers and gossip that surrounded me. Walking through crowded hallways, I faced the perceived judgment and stood up for myself and my right to an education.

In the real estate business, as well as in any other pursuit, you will encounter situations where you have to walk your own personal hallway. It may feel uncomfortable, especially when you put yourself in the public eye through marketing and social media platforms. People will always be there to make comments or pass judgments about you, but their opinions do not define you or your worth. Unless they are actively building their own business and are willing to step out of their comfort zones, their opinions hold no value in your journey.

Instead, focus on aligning with your own values, goals, and vision. Stay true to yourself and your purpose. Embrace the discomfort that comes with growth and push through it, knowing that it is part of the process. Surround yourself with supportive and like-minded people who understand the challenges of entrepreneurship and are committed to their own personal growth. These are the people who will lift you up, celebrate your successes, and provide guidance and encouragement along the way.

Your journey is unique, and not everyone will understand or support it. That's okay. Stay focused on your why, believe in yourself, and keep moving forward despite any external judgments or opinions. The only opinions that truly matter are those of the people who genuinely care about you and your success. Trust in yourself and your abilities, and don't let the fear of others' judgments hold you back from reaching your full potential.

People commonly worry about what others think of them, but this mindset can sabotage progress and success. Drawing from personal experiences, such as navigating judgments during my teenage pregnancy, I've learned the importance of staying true to myself and focusing on personal growth. Embrace discomfort as a part of the journey, surround yourself with supportive people, and prioritize your own values and goals. Ultimately, the opinions of others who do not understand or support your path should not hold you back from pursuing your dreams. Stay strong, believe in yourself, and forge ahead with confidence.

I love the exercise I introduced to my team earlier this year. I had each member write down whose opinion about them mattered most to them on a one-inch by one-inch piece of paper. It was a powerful way to help them recognize whose opinions truly matter and then prioritize their own self-worth. By writing down the names of the people whose opinions hold significance, it helped create clarity and focus and shed the egotistic portion of themselves which, in turn, enabled them to find strength in showing up and being seen by others.

My team members were initially puzzled by the size of the paper. This highlights the importance of understanding that the number of people whose opinions truly matter is relatively small. We often get caught up in worrying about what everyone thinks of us, when in reality, only a handful of people's opinions should have a significant impact on our lives.

The question of who your people would be in a challenging situation is thought-provoking. It forces you to reflect on the core relationships and support systems that truly matter. One of the most important names that should be on that paper is your own. Recognizing your own self-worth and trusting in your own abilities is essential for personal growth and success.

Interestingly, I observed that none of my team members included themselves on the paper. This was a powerful realization because it highlighted the need for self-esteem and personal growth. It reminded us that we must value ourselves and believe in our own potential before seeking validation from others. By placing their own names on the paper, your team members will acknowledge their worth and recognize the importance of prioritizing their own opinions and beliefs.

It was inspiring to see the growth and progress my team made, both personally and professionally, as they revisited the exercise the following year. Seeing their names on one side and only a few other names on the other demonstrated their increased confidence and understanding of their own value. They came to recognize their own power and the significance of their own opinions in their personal and professional journeys.

This exercise serves as a powerful reminder that we should not let the opinions of others define us or hold us back. By valuing ourselves, prioritizing our own growth, and surrounding ourselves with a select few whose opinions truly matter, we can navigate challenges, make confident decisions, and strive for success.

Including your own name on that tiny piece of paper reminds you of your personal power and the importance of self-esteem. As you revisit the exercise of using your own one-inch by one-inch paper, you will literally see your personal growth, confidence, and a deeper understanding of your own value. It is a wonderful reminder for all of us to prioritize ourselves and believe in our own potential as we navigate life and pursue success.

It is true that not everyone is going to like you, and that can be a challenging reality to accept. As a real estate professional, you will inevitably encounter situations where you have to relay messages on behalf of your clients that may not be well-received by other agents or their clients. Being a good negotiator and helping your clients achieve their goals requires you to navigate these challenging conversations with tact and professionalism.

You cannot please everyone, and that's okay. Your role is to advocate for your clients and work toward their best interests. Keep your values and goals in check in these situations. When you stay true to your principles, your actions will align with your clients' objectives and you will maintain your professional integrity.

It can be helpful to think of your personal and professional growth as a journey, like a toddler learning to walk. Just as we would not expect a toddler to run before they could walk, we should not expect instant success or universal approval in our careers without first learning the essential steps and putting them into daily practice. Instead, focus on nurturing your knowledge, skills, and relationships—the root system of your growth. Continuously seek opportunities to expand your expertise and deepen your understanding of the industry. By investing in your own growth and development, you can lay a strong foundation for your success.

Building a successful career in real estate takes time and dedication. Like a seed that grows into a plant and eventually a tall, well-rooted tree, your progress may be gradual but steady. Embrace the journey and focus on continuously nourishing yourself with knowledge and experience. As you grow, you will gain confidence and expertise that will enable you to navigate difficult situations and make a positive impact on your clients' lives.

Your own experiences, story, and personal growth will shape your journey in the industry. Success and growth are not defined by a single win or loss, but rather by the continuous progress and learning you achieve over time.

Each negotiation, every victory, and even the setbacks you encounter are valuable snapshots and moments in your career. They provide opportunities for growth, learning, and self-reflection. Celebrate your wins, learn from your losses, and use them as stepping stones to propel yourself forward.

Take a deep breath and appreciate every milestone and achievement along the way. Acknowledge the progress you have made, whether it's securing a successful deal, receiving positive feedback from clients, or expanding your knowledge and skills. These are all important markers of your growth and development.

At the same time, it is crucial to maintain perspective. Recognize that these moments are just part of your overall journey and not the sole measure of your abilities. Your career in real estate is a continuous process of growth, and each experience contributes to your professional development.

As you navigate the ups and downs of the industry, trust your instincts and rely on your own radar to guide you. Embrace the lessons and insights gained from each interaction and transaction and use them to refine your approach and enhance your abilities.

Ultimately, your career in real estate is a personal and unique journey. As you embrace the wins and learn from the losses, stay focused on your long-term growth and success. Your ability to recognize your own value and measure your progress will be a powerful tool in navigating the ever-changing landscape of the industry.

Being your own cheerleader and staying humble are essential qualities in the industry. While competition is inherent in the business, maintaining a balanced ego and genuine humility will greatly benefit your relationships with clients, competitors, and other professionals involved in deals.

Understanding yourself from the inside out allows you to avoid letting your ego dictate your actions and interactions. Ego often stems from external validation, such as monetary achievements or conforming to societal expectations, but true authenticity comes from aligning your actions with your core values and presenting yourself honestly to the world.

When we hide our true selves, our egos take control and can lead us to exaggerate our abilities and skills. This sets unrealistic expectations for clients and peers and creates a sense of dissonance within us. True success and fulfillment come from being genuine rather than trying to portray an inflated image of ourselves.

In the age of social media, much of what we see is curated and often highlights only the positive aspects of people's lives. Comparing ourselves to these edited versions of reality can be detrimental to our self-esteem. Real life is filled with challenges, responsibilities, and the daily grind that is often unseen in those picture-perfect moments.

Embracing authenticity means being honest about the ups and downs, the challenges and victories, and the everyday struggles that we all face. By staying real and sharing your genuine experiences, you create a connection with others that is based on truth and relatability. This builds trust and strengthens your relationships with clients and colleagues.

So, as you navigate the industry, keep your ego in check and embrace humility. Stay true to yourself, be transparent about your journey, and focus on building meaningful connections based on authenticity and trust. In doing so, you will attract the right clients and cultivate a reputation as a trustworthy and genuine professional.

Understanding the role of ego in your business is important. For some people, ego can serve as a motivator that drives them to elevate their status and step out of their comfort zone. If this resonates with you, examine how ego influences your decision-making process. If your ego-driven motivations align with self-promotion, expansion, and leading a team, channel that energy into productive avenues while remaining focused on continuous learning and personal growth.

Approaching your business with an open mind and an open heart allows you to stay honest with yourself and others. It is perfectly acceptable to acknowledge that you may not have all the answers from day one. Transparency and humility go a long way in building trust with clients. When you show up without ego and maintain a sense of curiosity and a commitment to personal growth, you attract and maintain closer connections with people. Being genuine and vulnerable, even when admitting that you haven't got all the answers, fosters stronger relationships and demonstrates your dedication to serving your clients' best interests.

Our egos often act as superficial barriers designed to shield us from past wounds and disappointments. When it comes to building a new foundation for yourself and your business, allow your ego to take a backseat. By shelving your ego and embracing humility, you create space for personal and professional growth, which paves the way for authentic connections, valuable learning experiences, and long-term success.

So, as you navigate your real estate journey, keep in mind the impact of ego on your decisions and interactions. Embrace humility, stay committed to learning, and remain curious about the world around you. By doing so, you will create an environment conducive to personal and professional development while building strong and meaningful connections with those around you.

CHAPTER SEVEN
Getting Out of Your Own Way

"Embrace your vulnerabilities, accept yourself as you are, and focus on the value you bring to the table."
—**Marcia Bergen**

CHAPTER SUMMARY

This chapter synthesized critical concepts in personal and professional growth, authenticity, and effective marketing in the context of the real estate industry. It underscored the importance of vulnerability, self-acceptance, and the embracing of one's unique traits and experiences as cornerstones in building authentic relationships and trust with clients. The text highlighted the significance of a clear vision, perseverance, and an authentic business persona while embracing changes, especially in the digital age. I discussed effective marketing strategies and conflict management, intertwined with an exploration of personal experiences and the significance of staying true to oneself. The chapter stressed that success is not measured in individual victories or losses but in continuous development and learning from each negotiation, victory, and setback. I delved into the role of ego, advocating for authenticity, humility, and transparency in all interactions while acknowledging that ego can be beneficial if properly channeled.

REFLECTION QUESTIONS

1. Who are the front-row cheerleaders in your life? Why is their support and opinion important to you?

2. Have you encountered individuals who are uncomfortable with your growth and success? Why do you think that is? How do you deal with this?

3. What are some of the "freckles" in your life that you've learned to embrace?

4. How do you feel about putting yourself out there in today's digital landscape?

5. In what ways has your ego influenced your decision-making process? Has this been beneficial or detrimental?

SCENARIOS

Scenario 1: Sarah is a newly licensed real estate agent who's afraid of criticism from seasoned agents. What must she do to successfully navigate through self-doubt and the inevitable criticism she will encounter in her career?

Scenario 2: Imagine you're a real estate professional who needs to discuss price reductions with sellers. Use the techniques discussed in this chapter, including data-driven arguments and clear communication, to handle this potentially sensitive conversation.

TO-DO LIST

- Perform the "one-inch by one-inch" paper exercise to identify whose opinions truly matter to you.
- Practice putting yourself in front of the camera and getting comfortable onscreen. Start by writing a simple script that introduces you and shoot a short video. Watch, take notes, make adjustments, and try it again in different ways until you see your persona emerge on the screen. Get feedback from the people whose names you wrote on the one-by-one-inch paper.
- Create a "branded" (see previous lesson) social media post for a platform that you use that aligns with your target audience's values and interests. Experiment with adapting the post for different platforms.

- Research and identify effective marketing strategies that could benefit your business.
- Identify potential partners or collaborators in your field and brainstorm ideas for joint projects.

STEP-BY-STEP INSTRUCTIONS
1. Complete the chapter reading.
2. Work through the reflection questions and scenarios.
3. Complete the to-do list.
4. Review your goals. Are you still on track?
5. Review previous lessons and continue synthesizing what you have learned into your business and professional persona.

TIPS AND TAKEAWAYS
- Regularly self-reflect on your actions and choices to ensure that they align with your authentic self.
- Surround yourself with positive influences and cheerleaders who fuel your motivation.
- Consistently deliver valuable and relevant content to connect with your audience.
- Use a data-driven approach when negotiating or managing conflicts.
- Regularly practice and internalize scripting techniques for better communication.
- Keep a journal of your wins, losses, and lessons learned in your real estate journey.

Your own takeaways:

- _____
  _____
- _____
  _____
- _____
  _____

CHAPTER EIGHT
What Is Your Value Proposition?

"Good character is more to be
praised than outstanding talent."
—John C. Maxwell

By definition, value proposition is the full mix of benefits or economic value that a company promises to deliver to consumers who buy their products or services. It is part of a company's overall marketing strategy which differentiates its brand and fully positions it in the market. A value proposition summarizes why a customer should buy a product or use a service. A well-presented and concise value proposition has the potential to convince the consumer that it will offer more value or better solve a problem for them relative to other offerings, thus turning the consumer into a customer or client. In business, real estate included, consumers are flooded with options and different value proposition. Each business promises that they can deliver a better service.

In such a competitive landscape, companies must clearly articulate their value proposition to stand out from the crowd. Relying solely on outstanding talent or superior products is no longer enough; businesses must also demonstrate their character and the unique value they bring to the table.

When crafting a value proposition, consider the needs and desires of the target audience. What problems are they facing? What solutions are they seeking? By addressing these questions, companies can tailor their value proposition to directly address the pain points of their potential customers.

A strong value proposition goes beyond simply listing the features of a product or service. It delves into the benefits and outcomes customers expect to receive. It communicates the value that will be added to their lives or businesses if they choose a particular offering. This could be in the form of time saved, money saved, increased efficiency, improved quality, or enhanced convenience.

Moreover, a value proposition should highlight the unique selling points that set a company apart from its competitors. What makes the business special? Is it the exceptional customer service, the innovative technology, or the commitment to sustainability? By identifying and emphasizing these differentiators, a company can position itself as the preferred choice for customers who align with its values.

The tone of a value proposition should be persuasive and compelling. It should inspire confidence in the audience and convey a sense of trustworthiness. Customers need to feel that they can rely on the promises being made and that the company has their best interests at heart.

A value proposition is not a static entity. Like your why, it should evolve and adapt as market conditions change and customer preferences shift. Regularly reassessing and refining the value proposition ensures that it remains relevant and effective in capturing the attention and loyalty of customers.

Ultimately, a well-crafted value proposition can make all the difference in a company's success. It has the power to differentiate a business from its competitors, attract customers, and build long-lasting relationships. By focusing on the benefits, unique selling points, and customer needs, companies can create a value proposition that resonates with their target audience and drives growth.

While outstanding talent may be commendable, the good character of a company, reflected in its value proposition, is what truly sets it apart. By clearly articulating the benefits and unique value it offers, a business can position itself as the preferred choice for customers, which leads to success in a competitive marketplace. The key to a compelling value proposition lies in understanding the customer, addressing their pain points, and delivering on promises.

When considering your value proposition as the foundation of your business, draw parallels with the construction industry. Just as different types of foundations offer unique benefits and stability to a building, a well-defined value proposition provides the groundwork for a successful business.

Similar to selecting a foundation material in construction, crafting a value proposition involves careful consideration of various factors. One must analyze the target market, understand customer needs and preferences, and evaluate the competitive landscape. This research helps determine the most effective value proposition that will differentiate the business and attract customers.

Different foundations have specific characteristics, so a value proposition should possess certain qualities, too. It should be clear, concise, and easily understood by the target audience. It must communicate the unique value the business offers and state the benefits customers can expect to receive.

In the construction industry, one must assess whether a foundation takes in water or if it was designed to do so. Similarly, a value proposition should address potential challenges or pain points customers face. It should offer solutions or advantages that set the business apart from competitors.

The stability and longevity of a foundation are critical considerations, therefore, a value proposition should be durable and adaptable. It must be able to withstand changes in the market and evolving customer demands. Regularly evaluating and refining the value proposition ensures its relevance and effectiveness over time.

Just as different foundation materials have varying repair capabilities and lifespans, a value proposition should be flexible and easily modifiable. This allows businesses to respond to feedback, market trends, and customer preferences. By being open to modifications, a business can ensure its value proposition remains aligned with the needs and expectations of its target audience.

Moreover, like a strong foundation, a compelling value proposition instills confidence and trust. It should demonstrate the company's integrity and commitment to delivering on its promises. Customers should feel assured that by choosing the business, they will receive the stated benefits and value.

In a saturated industry such as real estate, where numerous experienced agents coexist alongside a constant influx of new entrants, everyone must recognize the significance of offering unique value in order to thrive and establish a successful business. Imagine a local marketplace where 100,000 transactions occur each year and 2,500 agents are already operating in the area. This scenario highlights the need for new agents or business owners to understand that they must actively capture a portion of the market share to build a viable business. This means you must be willing and capable of capturing of a portion of the existing market by taking business that belongs to someone else. When you take market share from someone else, you are essentially taking business away from another agent. You can do this when you differentiate yourself and create opportunities that were previously unavailable in the local market.

To stand out and capture market share, new agents or entrepreneurs must identify and communicate their unique value proposition. This involves understanding the needs and pain points of their target audience and developing solutions that surpass the offerings of existing competitors. For instance, an agent could specialize in a particular niche market, such as luxury properties or first-time homebuyers. By becoming an expert in that specific area, they can provide specialized knowledge and personalized services to create a value proposition that appeals to a distinct segment of the market.

Furthermore, offering additional services or going above and beyond what is typically expected can help create opportunities that differentiate an agent from the competition. This could involve providing comprehensive market analyses, offering innovative marketing strategies, or leveraging technology to enhance the buying or selling experience.

Building strong relationships and a solid reputation within the community is another avenue for creating market share. By actively engaging with potential clients through networking events, community involvement, and leveraging social media platforms, agents establish themselves as trustworthy and reliable professionals.

Understanding the importance of offering value is essential for new agents or entrepreneurs looking to establish their business in a saturated market. By recognizing the need to take or make market share, and by offering unique services, specialized expertise, exceptional customer experiences, and actively engaging with the community, agents create opportunities that differentiate themselves and build a successful business in their local marketplace.

In the realm of professional endeavors, having a clear sense of self and a defined understanding of your target clientele are fundamental components of success. When you are armed with this knowledge, you are ready to embark on a journey of introspection and delve deeper into your own capabilities. Amidst this introspection, a crucial question emerges: What unique offerings can I provide to set me apart from other agents in the field?

It is an undeniable truth that you can potentially offer the same services and products as other agents in your industry; however, the differentiating factor lies in how you present these offerings. By infusing your own personal dialogue and relatability into the equation, you can present a familiar experience in a refreshing and distinctive package. One might envision this concept as giving a gift—a gift that mirrors those offered by others—but with a twist. It's like wrapping the same present in eye-catching paper adorned with ribbons and bows. This approach breathes new life into what might seem like a well-trodden path by captivating the attention of your potential clients and setting you apart from the competition.

To further illustrate the importance of this distinction, let's examine a scenario involving two agents. Agent 1 diligently knocks on 100 doors, expending significant effort and time, only to find that their endeavors yield zero leads. On the other hand, Agent 2 knocks on 50 doors and achieves a remarkable outcome of generating five valuable leads. What sets these two agents apart? The answer lies in the concept of a value proposition.

A value proposition is the unique blend of offerings, benefits, and experiences that an agent brings to the table. It encapsulates the essence of what makes them distinct and valuable in the eyes of potential clients. In the scenario described above, the Agent 2 possessed a compelling value proposition that resonated with their audience, which led to a higher success rate despite making fewer attempts.

The concept of a value proposition can be likened to a personal brand. Just as individuals develop their own unique brand identities, agents must cultivate their own distinct value propositions. This involves understanding and articulating the core strengths, expertise, and added value they bring to the table. By effectively communicating this value proposition, agents position themselves as indispensable partners to their clients.

In a saturated marketplace, standing out can be a formidable challenge; however, by recognizing that the same services can be delivered with a fresh perspective and personal touch, agents can leverage their individuality to carve a niche for themselves. Clients are not merely seeking a product or service; they are also seeking a connection—an emotional bond that resonates with their own aspirations, values, and desires. By infusing your own voice, personality, and relatability into your interactions, you create an authentic and engaging experience that sets you apart from the competition.

When embarking on a career in real estate, it is completely acceptable to embrace a learning curve and initially model your behavior and offerings after other successful agents. As you gain experience and develop a clearer understanding of your own capabilities and business vision, explore what unique contributions you can bring to the table and how you envision your business flourishing. In my personal journey, I have adopted a strategy of repackaging my offerings and introducing new elements to my business on an annual basis, thereby staying relevant and continually improving my services.

When I first entered the real estate business, I made the decision to offer home staging as an added benefit for my clients, at no additional cost. I loaded up my SUV with art and decor from my own walls and repurposed them to enhance the aesthetic appeal of my clients' homes. I would go to great lengths using possessions I already had at my disposal. I took furniture from my own living room, removed drapes from my own rods, and used any other accessories or items necessary to present my clients' homes in the best possible light.

As a result of my resourcefulness and dedication to providing exceptional service, there were times when my children would come home and humorously inquire which of my listed properties ended up with the cereal from our kitchen cupboard. While this may be a slight exaggeration, it is true that we occasionally found ourselves having meals at the kitchen island while one of my listings on the market was furnished with our dining table and chairs. I was willing to make these unconventional sacrifices because I believed it was necessary to go the extra mile to attract more business and ultimately sustain the success of my venture.

In the early stages of a real estate career, it is natural to rely on the tried-and-true methods employed by others in the field. It provides a solid foundation and allows you to learn from those who have already achieved success. As you grow more confident in your abilities and gain a deeper understanding of your own strengths, the time will come when you must infuse your unique touch and offerings into your business model. For me, this involved a commitment to continual growth and innovation. Each year, I strive to introduce a fresh element to my business that sets me apart from my competitors. This could be a new service, a unique marketing strategy, or an innovative approach to client engagement. By reinventing and enhancing my offerings, I remain relevant and stay ahead of the curve in an ever-evolving industry.

While the early days of my career demanded personal sacrifices and creative problem-solving, they ultimately paved the way for my success. By pushing boundaries and embracing unconventional methods, I was able to demonstrate my commitment to delivering exceptional service and going above and beyond for my clients.

Over the past five years or so, staging has made significant gains in popularity and relevance; however, prior to this surge, the options for staging services were limited, and the associated costs were often prohibitive, so it was seldom included as a standard service. Fortunately for me, given my background and expertise in home improvement and design, incorporating staging became a seamless addition to my array of offerings.

In the present landscape, there exists a multitude of staging companies to choose from, and each offers various levels of service tailored to individual client needs. As part of my value proposition, I now include staging as a core component, but my approach to staging evolves significantly over time.

The inclusion of staging in my business model is just one example of what a value proposition can encompass. It serves as a tangible demonstration of how I have used this service to differentiate myself from competitors. By incorporating staging as an integral part of my overall package, I am able to offer clients a comprehensive and compelling experience that sets me apart.

In the realm of real estate, a value proposition is more than just a slogan or a catchphrase. It is a strategic approach that defines the unique benefits, offerings, and experiences an agent brings to the table. It is the culmination of factors that make one's services and expertise invaluable to clients. By identifying and leveraging these differentiating factors, agents can position themselves as the go-to professionals in their field.

The concept of a value proposition extends beyond the example of staging. It encompasses various elements such as personalized marketing strategies, niche specialization, exceptional customer service, or innovative technology integration. The key is to identify what sets you apart from the competition and use those unique strengths to create a compelling and irresistible offering for clients.

By offering different levels of options for sellers, I have not only witnessed a significant increase in the volume of my business, but also a remarkable 40 percent rise in gross commission when comparing the exact number of transactions this year to the previous year.

A 40 percent increase in commission is undoubtedly substantial when considering the precise number of deals that were transacted. So, how did I achieve this feat? I approached my business from a clear financial perspective and made the strategic decision to provide sellers with a diverse range of services, aiming to simplify their experience and enhance transparency.

To achieve this, I offer three levels of listing packages, each clearly outlining the inclusions and offerings. All of my commission packages ensure that the buyer's agents receive market-standard commissions, while simultaneously offering my clients three levels of services which range from two to four percent solely on the listing end. What I discovered through this change in strategy was that most of my clients opted for the higher two options. This reveals an important truth: clients are willing to pay for value when they perceive that value to extend beyond monetary considerations.

In my base listing package, I provide what the majority of my competitors offer, supplemented by additional marketing strategies that are fully transparent in their projected benefits for the sellers. For example, I demonstrate to potential clients how incorporating Google or social media ads can expose their home to an additional 8,000 to 16,000 people beyond the reach of the Multiple Listing System alone. Additionally, I include professional cleaning services and a communication guarantee that ensures a higher level of customer satisfaction.

Moving up to the second listing package, my clients have the option of either partially or fully staging their home. To illustrate the effectiveness of this approach, I present my sellers with data comparing a home sold using staging techniques to one that was listed without staging, despite appearing to have similar market advantages. By showcasing this comparison, I highlight why the staged home did not achieve the higher sale price that it seemingly should have commanded in a competitive market.

The third option that I offer clients involves the opportunity to renovate or improve their home at my expense, up to one percent of their property's value. This investment is aimed at enhancing the final listing and sale price. Of course, such cases involve additional paperwork to ensure that these funds will be reimbursed to me should a seller decide to remove their home from the market.

What I have discovered is that most individuals appreciate the opportunity to customize their real estate experience. This approach also grants people the flexibility to undertake some aspects of the process themselves, or alternatively, to place value on delegating tasks to myself and my team.

In summary, by offering a range of options to sellers, I have experienced a significant increase in both business volume and gross commission. By allowing clients to tailor their experience to their specific needs, I provide a sense of transparency, personalization, and value that resonates with them. This approach has proven successful and has attracted clients who appreciate the opportunity to customize their real estate journey and recognize the advantages of investing in services that extend beyond mere monetary considerations.

One common misconception in the real estate business is that cutting commission is a value proposition. The truth is that negotiating your own commission with sellers can undermine your credibility when it comes to negotiating the value of their home. By engaging in commission negotiations with buyer's agents, you inadvertently send a message that not only compromises your ability to negotiate effectively, but also devalues the entire industry.

Once you outline your business plan, you might realize that your goals and values are unique to you and do not align exactly with those of your competitors. Your first and foremost value proposition should be yourself. You possess the ability to offer a higher level of knowledge and expertise to your clients. You are capable of delivering exceptional communication throughout the buying or selling process. You have the skills to create a detailed marketing plan when selling a property. Additionally, you can establish a platform that keeps your clients well-informed about market conditions and expertly guide them through financing, property selection, and ultimately, the home-purchasing process.

Developing a clear understanding of your value proposition and leveraging it to create a differentiated experience for your clients is a powerful strategy. By doing so, you provide exceptional service and facilitate the efficient and rapid expansion of your business.

Your value proposition defines the unique benefits and offerings that set you apart from competitors. It encompasses your expertise, skills, and personalized approach to serving clients. When you deeply understand your value proposition, you can effectively communicate it to potential clients, demonstrating why they should choose you over others in the market.

In essence, you are the true value proposition when you present yourself fully to your clients. By being present and actively engaged with your clients, you demonstrate your commitment to their needs. Timely and effective communication is key, as it fosters trust and transparency. By delivering exceptional knowledge, communication, and guidance, and making yourself readily available to your clients throughout their real estate journey, you establish yourself as a reliable and trusted advisor.

One valuable lesson I learned early in my career, during a real estate conference, was the impact of a seemingly small task: answering your phone. When I share this insight with new or seasoned agents in my office, it often elicits chuckles or even eye rolls. Nevertheless, statistics demonstrate the critical importance of responding promptly to leads. The longer you wait—whether it be a minute, an hour, six hours, or even a full day—the more likely it is that the lead has already searched and contacted someone else. As a new agent or business owner, losing even a single lead can be detrimental. It means relinquishing potential market share to someone else, and it highlights how swiftly business can slip through your fingers.

To combat this, I have implemented a practice of promptly responding to calls and emails, even if I am unavailable at that exact moment. In such cases, I respond with a message conveying my gratitude for their contact and inform them that I am currently with a client. Additionally, I provide a specific time frame, such as 10, 20, or 30 minutes, within which I will call them back. When it comes to email inquiries, I reply immediately with a realistic timeline for my response. By following through on these commitments, I establish the first building blocks of trust with potential clients.

Delivering on what you promise is paramount in gaining and maintaining people's attention and respect. By promptly returning calls and emails, you demonstrate respect for their time and show that you prioritize their needs. This initial step of responsiveness lays the foundation for building a solid relationship based on trust.

In today's fast-paced world, where instant gratification is often expected, promptly addressing inquiries sets you apart from the vast majority of agents. It shows your dedication, professionalism, and commitment to providing exceptional service. Furthermore, it increases the likelihood of converting leads into clients, as they are more likely to remain engaged and receptive to your guidance and expertise.

Never underestimate the power of answering your phone and responding promptly to inquiries. It may seem like a simple task, but its impact on your business growth and success should not be underestimated. By adopting this practice, you position yourself as a reliable and attentive agent, capture the attention and respect of potential clients, and ultimately secure their trust as you guide them through their real estate journey.

Understanding and offering unique value attracts and retains clients. Believe in the value you bring, as your clients will perceive it in the same way. Merely having a license and framed certificate will not compel people to choose you as their agent. To truly thrive in this business, you must invest time in understanding your purpose and the difference you want to make for your clients.

You can offer value to your clients in various ways. One example is to host buyer meetings before showing them any listings. During these meetings, you explain the entire buying process and walk them through the necessary forms and components of an offer to purchase. Show them current listings and recently sold properties within their desired price range and neighborhoods to help them understand what homes they can expect to view. Educate them about financing, including when payments start and how to monitor market fluctuations in interest rates. For instance, if interest rates decrease, homeowners may want to consider refinancing their mortgage at a lower rate, even if it involves paying a penalty. Conversely, if interest rates are predicted to rise, engaging in a "blend and extend" strategy to secure a favorable rate for a longer term may be advantageous.

The buying process can be stressful, particularly during the paperwork stage and when working with lawyers. Drawing on my experience as a real estate paralegal, I explain additional costs involved, such as the provincial tax known as Land Transfer Tax. Other expenses may include legal fees, mortgage registration costs, title insurance policy fees, photocopying, file fees, courier charges, and utility or tax adjustments. Providing buyers with an estimate of closing costs (usually around two percent of the purchase price) helps them prepare financially.

One significant benefit of meeting buyers before viewing properties is to establish a foundation of trust from the outset so you can reduce the amount of time spent on property showings before they make a purchase decision.

Another way to offer value is by creating an exceptional client experience. For instance, prepare children's care packages with crayons, coloring pages, puzzle games, granola bars, and water, and include a personalized note for each child. This gesture leaves a positive impression and shows that you genuinely care about their family's needs, and it allows parents to focus on their goal of purchasing property as opposed to tending to parenting responsibilities.

When clients fly in from out of town, going the extra mile by offering to pick them up and drive them between properties can save them the hassle of renting a vehicle. Additionally, preparing a basket with snacks, water, listings, and neighborhood maps, along with branded pens for taking notes, demonstrates attentiveness and professionalism.

By delivering on your value proposition, you provide an exceptional experience that exceeds client expectations. This exceptional experience becomes a catalyst for positive word-of-mouth referrals and client loyalty, which drives the organic growth of your business. Satisfied clients become brand ambassadors who advocate for your services and attract new clients to your doorstep.

Furthermore, a well-defined value proposition enables you to streamline your business operations and target your marketing efforts more effectively. By understanding the specific needs and desires of your target audience, you can tailor your services, communication, and marketing strategies to address their pain points and offer solutions that resonate with them. This targeted approach ensures that your business reaches the right clients at the right time, while maximizing your efficiency and minimizing wasted resources.

Additionally, a differentiated experience that stems from a strong value proposition helps you stand out in a crowded marketplace. It positions you as a trusted expert and go-to professional in your field. Clients are more likely to choose you when they recognize the unique value and benefits you bring to the table. This differentiation allows you to attract clients who are aligned with your values and appreciate the specific expertise and services you offer.

As your business grows more efficiently and quickly due to your exceptional value proposition, you can leverage this momentum to expand your reach and diversify your services. Satisfied clients are more likely to engage in repeat business and refer you to others, which opens new opportunities and expands your client base.

Embrace your value proposition as a guiding principle and watch your business flourish.

CHAPTER EIGHT
What is Your Value Proposition?

*"Clients are willing to pay for value when they perceive
that value to extend beyond monetary considerations."*
—Marcia Bergen

CHAPTER SUMMARY

In this text, I discussed the role of a compelling value proposition in the business landscape by drawing on my experiences in the real estate industry. I emphasized that a value proposition is not a static concept, but rather a dynamic one that encapsulates the unique benefits, expertise, offerings, and experiences that set me apart in a competitive market. I shared my innovative strategy of providing various levels of services to sellers that have led to a substantial increase in both my business volume and commission. I debunked the common misconception that reducing commission equates to a value proposition. Instead, I stressed that it is an agent's personal skills, knowledge, and exceptional communication that constitute the true value proposition. Furthermore, I underscored the significance of prompt communication, honoring commitments, and providing genuine care to clients beyond monetary transactions as key components in building trust and ensuring client satisfaction.

REVIEW
What is a Value Proposition?

A value proposition is the comprehensive combination of benefits or economic value that a company promises to deliver to consumers who purchase their products or services.

A value proposition is the key to a company's overall marketing strategy that distinguishes a brand and effectively positions it within the market. It articulates why a customer should choose one service over another, and how that company can provide superior value or more effectively resolve a problem compared to competitors.

A VALUE PROPOSITION SHOULD:

- Address potential challenges or pain points encountered by customers.
- Offer solutions or advantages that distinguish the business from competitors.
- Remain durable and adaptable, and able to withstand changes in the market and evolving customer demands.
- Demonstrate the company's integrity and commitment to fulfilling its promises.
- Encompass a business owner's expertise, skills, and personalized approach to serving clients.

REFLECTION QUESTIONS

1. Think about your value proposition. What would that include?
2. How can you use your personal strengths and skills to differentiate yourself from the competition?
3. How do you demonstrate to your clients that you value them beyond monetary considerations?
4. Why is it necessary for a value proposition to evolve over time?

SCENARIOS

Scenario 1: John is a real estate agent struggling to differentiate himself in a competitive market. He decides to focus on his unique value proposition, which is his detailed knowledge of the local area and his exceptional customer service. In what ways can John leverage or enhance his unique value proposition to reach his goals?

Scenario 2: Laura is a real estate agent with a background in creative communications. She is known for her prompt responses, her personable and empathetic approach to communicating with clients, and her killer sense of humor; however, Laura realizes she can improve her client service by offering more value. How can Laura leverage or enhance her unique skills to add more to her value proposition?

TO-DO LIST
Keep your buyer persona from Chapter 4 in mind as you complete these tasks:
- Identify the unique selling points of your business (your strengths and unique traits).
- Analyze the value propositions of your competitors. Identify what they are doing well and areas where you can offer something unique or better.
- Craft your value proposition. Based on the above steps, create a concise, clear, and compelling value proposition. It should address your target audience's needs and clearly highlight the unique value your business provides.
- Review your value proposition regularly and make adjustments as necessary.

STEP-BY-STEP INSTRUCTIONS
1. Read through the chapter.
2. Reflect on what you have read by working through the reflection questions and scenarios.
3. Complete the tasks on your to-do list.
4. Review your goals, and then consider how your value proposition aligns with what you are aiming to achieve.
5. Review your previous lessons and continue to do research and develop your skills.

TIPS AND TAKEAWAYS
- Learn your audience's needs and pain points to create a compelling value proposition.

- Stay relevant: Your value proposition should evolve with changing market conditions and customer preferences.
- Be clear and concise: Your value proposition should be easy to understand and communicate the unique value your business provides.
- Deliver on your promises: A strong value proposition is only as good as your ability to deliver on it.
- Transparency and personalization are key to creating compelling offerings for clients.
- Prompt and effective communication builds trust with clients.
- Find ways to offer value that extend beyond monetary considerations.

Your own takeaways:

- _____
  _____
- _____
  _____
- _____
  _____

CHAPTER NINE
How Do You Get Your Value Proposition
Out to Build a Stable Business?

"I alone cannot change the world, but I can cast a
stone across the waters to create many ripples."
—Mother Teresa

Reflecting on past romantic relationships, one notable insight that stands out to me, as a woman in her fifties, is the understanding that a strong relationship is not solely built on grand, occasional gestures. Rather, it is the result of consistent small gestures and considerations that we make for one another.

This realization holds true not only in personal relationships but also in the context of business. Building a successful business is not solely reliant on occasional grand acts or impressive displays, but the cumulative effect of consistent small gestures and considerations toward clients, customers, and partners.

In a business context, these small gestures manifest in a lot of ways. It could be as simple as promptly returning calls and emails, actively listening to clients' needs and concerns, or going the extra mile to provide personalized solutions. It might involve remembering important details about clients' preferences or situations, demonstrating genuine care and empathy, and showing appreciation for their support and trust.

Consistency is key in building a strong business relationship. Just as a romantic partner appreciates consistent acts of love and consideration, clients and customers value a consistent experience that meets or exceeds their expectations. By delivering high-quality products, services, and interactions, we establish trust and loyalty with our customers to create long-term relationships, which increases the likelihood of referrals and repeat business.

Moreover, cultivating strong business relationships requires ongoing efforts to understand and adapt to the evolving needs and preferences of our target audience. This means staying informed about industry trends, continuously improving our skills and knowledge, and actively seeking feedback from clients to ensure we meet their expectations.

Ultimately, success in both personal relationships and business hinges on the understanding that it is the accumulation of small gestures and considerations that builds lasting connections. By nurturing relationships with care and continuously striving to meet clients' needs, we lay the foundation for long-term success and growth in our businesses.

So, as we reflect on the lessons learned from personal experiences, let us carry forward the understanding that lasting relationships, whether personal or professional, thrive on a foundation of small gestures and considerations. By embracing this principle, we cultivate strong and mutually beneficial connections that stand the test of time.

When aiming to establish a business that delivers results, construct a comprehensive business and marketing plan that incorporates a series of small, repetitive actions or tasks. These actions should be implemented on a regular basis, whether weekly, monthly, or annually, or a combination of all three.

By breaking down your business and marketing activities into manageable and recurring tasks, you create a structured framework that ensures continuous progress and growth. These small actions, when performed consistently, yield cumulative results and contribute to the overall success of your business.

Weekly tasks provide an excellent opportunity to engage with your target audience and maintain a consistent presence. These tasks can include activities such as creating and sharing valuable content through blog posts or social media, responding promptly to customer inquiries and messages, conducting outreach to potential clients, networking with industry professionals, and regularly reviewing and analyzing performance metrics to identify areas for improvement.

By dedicating time each week to these tasks, you are actively engaging with your audience, providing them with valuable information, and staying top of mind as a trusted real estate professional. These efforts will help build credibility and trust, which ultimately leads to stronger relationships and more opportunities for your business.

Moving on to monthly tasks, this is the ideal time frame to review and refine your strategies and processes. Take time to thoroughly analyze your marketing efforts and assess the effectiveness of different channels and campaigns. Look at key performance indicators such as website traffic, social media engagement, lead generation, and conversion rates. Evaluate customer feedback and testimonials to gain insights into what is resonating with your audience and what can be improved. Break down your social media posts to either five or seven recurring themes that define what your content will be on those days. For example, you might create your own personal or business hashtag such as Monday Motivation, Tuesday Testimonials or Friday Features. By creating themes to follow on a weekly basis, you take the stress out of finding new or relative content and have the ability to preplan your posts by setting aside one day a month to create and schedule the marketing. This will give you more time to focus on the other aspects of your business in order to generate more or nurture existing business.

Annual tasks provide an opportunity to take a broader perspective and set long-term goals for your business. Reflect on your achievements and challenges over the past year by celebrating your successes and identifying areas for improvement. Conduct a comprehensive review of your business performance by analyzing financials, client satisfaction, and overall growth.

Update your business plan, taking into account any changes in the market or industry trends. Set new objectives for the upcoming year, both in terms of business growth and personal development. Allocate time for professional development such as attending conferences or workshops, acquiring new skills or certifications, and staying updated on industry news and best practices.

By incorporating these weekly, monthly, and annual tasks into your business routine, you create a framework for growth and improvement. The regular engagement with your target audience, the analysis of your marketing efforts, and the setting of long-term goals enable you to adapt and thrive in a dynamic real estate industry. Success in real estate is not a one-time event, but a continuous journey of learning, adapting, and providing value to your clients.

The combination of these small, repetitive actions across different time frames creates a cohesive and continuous effort that propels your business forward. By adhering to this systematic approach, you establish a routine that fosters consistency, discipline, and productivity. It helps you stay focused on your goals and prevents important tasks from falling through the cracks.

To effectively execute your chosen strategies and ensure consistency in your marketing efforts, create a firm plan that outlines how you will allocate your time throughout the week. Here is a suggested approach to help you structure your time effectively:

Determine your weekly priorities. Start by identifying your most important tasks and goals for the week. This could include creating content for your newsletters, planning social media posts, conducting area farming activities, writing blog posts, or engaging in community sponsorships. Prioritize these tasks based on their impact and importance to your business.

By following a well-defined plan and remaining focused on your chosen strategies, you effectively allocate your time and resources to ensure proper execution and delivery of your marketing efforts. It is better to excel in a few chosen avenues than to spread yourself too thin across multiple strategies. Embrace the 90/10 rule and trust that through consistent effort and dedication, you will achieve the growth and success you desire in your real estate business.

I have built my business on three pillars: communication, planned marketing strategies, and fostering relationships with both current and potential clients. These pillars can be customized and adapted to align with your personal values, goals, and personality. I recommend focusing on three pillars because spreading yourself too thin across multiple areas can hinder your ability to establish a consistent and impactful presence.

When I initially entered the industry, I heavily relied on direct relationships and personal connections to spread the word about my new venture. In the first year, this approach proved effective as I enthusiastically shared my message of being a realtor with everyone I encountered; however, as the novelty wore off in my second year, my enthusiasm waned and resulted in a decline in business and sales. Although I was earning a decent income and covering my expenses, my business wasn't growing as I had envisioned.

Realizing the need for a change, I decided in my third year to attend a conference and seek guidance from a coach. This allowed me to gain insights on how to grow my business and develop a clear organizational and promotional strategy to foster consistency.

For me, consistency equates to stability. It is this stability that has enabled me to fully immerse myself in my business and commit to delivering a consistent message year after year. This commitment has played a vital role in the growth of my business and the trust I have built with clients.

Consistency in communication, marketing efforts, and relationship-building has allowed me to establish a strong foundation for my business. It has provided a sense of stability and reliability, both for myself and my clients. By delivering on my promises, maintaining regular contact with clients, and executing planned marketing strategies, I have been able to cultivate a growing and thriving business.

Starting a real estate career with limited resources can be daunting, but by focusing on the pillars of communication, planned marketing strategies, and fostering relationships, it is possible to overcome challenges and achieve growth. Consistency provides stability and allows your business to flourish. By committing to a consistent approach, you establish a strong presence, build trust, and ultimately create a successful and thriving business.

When considering the three pillars of marketing for your business, there are several examples you can explore. Each of these pillars can be customized to align with your vision and personal brand. By focusing on three pillars, you can avoid spreading yourself too thin. The following are examples of individual pillars of marketing:

Monthly Newsletters: Creating and distributing your own newsletters on a monthly basis can be a cost-effective way to provide value and showcase your expertise. These newsletters can include home maintenance tips, local market updates, and even personal touches like favorite recipes or restaurant recommendations. Use a branded template to deliver this content to your audience and establish yourself as a knowledgeable resource.

Area Farming: Area farming involves targeting a specific neighborhood or area with your marketing efforts. This can be achieved through blogging, postcards, flyers, bus bench ads, community sponsorships, and events. By marketing to a particular area, you position yourself as the go-to agent for that location; however, you must assess the feasibility and market dynamics of your specific area. In some cases, it may be more advantageous to keep your options open and explore opportunities across a broader scope.

Blogging: While it can be time-consuming, blogging is an effective way to share your real estate expertise, showcase your personality, and provide information to potential clients. Regularly posting blogs, whether biweekly or monthly, allows you to engage your audience, incorporate humor and business tips, and use visuals such as photos and videos to keep readers engaged.

Social Media Marketing: Leveraging social media platforms provides a low-cost or free opportunity to reinforce your brand and message. Ensure that everything you post aligns with your brand and maintains a professional tone. Adhering to the 80/20 rule—80 percent related to real estate, market conditions, and homeowner tips, and 20 percent related to your defined business personal life—helps strike the right balance. Tailor your content for each platform using blogs and newsletter content for LinkedIn, and everyday knowledge and behind-the-scenes glimpses for platforms like Facebook, TikTok, and Instagram.

Community Highlights: By connecting with local business owners and promoting their services, you establish yourself as an expert in specific neighborhoods while expanding your network. This also provides an excellent opportunity to create content for your social media platforms. You can feature different neighborhoods, showcase local businesses, and highlight community events. Building relationships with business owners allows you to tap into their network and attract potential clients.

Door Knocking: While initially intimidating, door knocking can be an effective way to meet homeowners and establish connections. To make it less daunting, come prepared with informative material and resources that can assist residents. For example, you can provide information about upcoming tax assessments, offer comparable sales data, and explain the appeal process. Another approach is to promote an exclusive open house for neighbors. Provide them with refreshments and the opportunity to learn more about the neighborhood and recent sales. By positioning yourself as a knowledgeable resource, you increase your chances of being considered when residents think of selling their property.

Cold Calling: While this is not everyone's preferred marketing tool, cold calling can yield results when done consistently and strategically. Allocate dedicated time each day to making five to ten calls to keep people informed about the current market status and offering your expertise and services. Persistence and a well-prepared pitch are key to making cold calling effective.

Expired Listings: Expired listings refer to properties that were previously listed on the Multiple Listing System but did not sell. By contacting the homeowners directly, you can showcase your unique value proposition, present recent sales data, and offer a fresh approach to selling their property. It is required by our legal commissions to include a disclaimer stating that you are not soliciting their business if they are currently under contract with another agent. Familiarize yourself with your listing presentation and be prepared to address any concerns or objections they may have.

For Sale by Owner (FSBO): FSBO properties present an opportunity to convert sellers who are attempting to sell their homes without an agent. This approach can be challenging, as some FSBO sellers may be hesitant to work with agents or have differing opinions on pricing. Many FSBO properties are often overpriced compared to market inventory or recent sales. Engaging with FSBO sellers requires effective communication to demonstrate the value you bring to the table and the ability to provide market insights to help them make informed decisions.

Community Sponsorships: While this marketing strategy may be dependent on your budget, it can be a valuable addition to an existing area farming approach. Sponsorships offer exposure and allow you to support local events or organizations; however, you must assess the return on investment and ensure that it aligns with your overall marketing plan.

Time is a finite resource, so use it wisely. If your current social circle is not generating business, consider expanding your network to include people who are more likely to engage with your services. Embrace social media platforms and use them effectively by understanding each platform's nuances and tailoring your content accordingly. Engage authentically with your connections by taking care to comment and connect in a meaningful way.

Additionally, prioritize consistency and commit to your chosen marketing strategies. The agents who dedicate themselves to their chosen pillars will likely achieve greater success than those who only partially commit.

To effectively execute your chosen strategies and ensure consistency in your marketing efforts, create a firm plan that outlines how you will allocate your time throughout the week. Here is a suggested approach to help structure your time effectively:

Start by identifying your most important tasks and goals for the week. This could include creating content for your newsletters, planning social media posts, conducting area farming activities, writing blog posts, or engaging in community sponsorships. Prioritize these tasks based on their impact and importance to your business.

Block dedicated time for each pillar by allocating specific time slots in your schedule for each of your chosen pillars. For example, you could set aside a block of time each week to write and distribute your newsletters, another block for blogging, and separate time for social media marketing, area farming, or door knocking. By assigning dedicated time to each pillar, each aspect of your marketing strategy receives proper attention and effort.

Develop a content calendar to help you plan and organize your content creation. This could include topics for your newsletters, blog posts, and social media posts. By mapping out your content in advance, you create a consistent flow of valuable information for your audience. While you can consider using tools or software to schedule and automate your social media posts, be mindful of the previous chapters wherein I discussed showing up differently for defined media outlets.

Regularly review and analyze the performance of your marketing efforts. Track metrics such as open rates for newsletters, engagement on social media, website traffic, or lead conversions. This data will provide insights into the effectiveness of your strategies and help you make informed decisions on how to refine and improve your marketing approach.

Based on the performance data and feedback from your audience, adjust and refine your plan. Stay flexible and open to experimentation, as different strategies may yield varying results. Use your analysis to identify areas of improvement and adapt your approach accordingly.

Stay focused on your brand strategy and vision: Throughout your marketing activities, keep your brand strategy and vision at the forefront. Ensure that your messaging and content align with your brand identity and values. Consistency in your communication and presentation will help reinforce your brand image and establish trust with your audience.

Building a successful business requires dedication, effort, and perseverance. Embrace the hustle by executing your marketing plan and staying committed to your chosen pillars. Trust the process and have confidence that your efforts will yield the desired results over time.

By following a well-defined plan and remaining focused on your chosen strategies, you can effectively allocate your time and resources to ensure consistent execution and delivery of your marketing efforts. It is better to excel in a few chosen pillars than to spread yourself too thin across multiple strategies. Trust that through consistent effort and dedication, you will achieve the business growth and success you desire.

Your commitment to focusing on your chosen pillars builds a business that delivers consistent performance and sales. It's natural for new business to experience fluctuations and waves, but by maintaining a disciplined approach to your marketing efforts, you can minimize or even eliminate these fluctuations and establish a stable and reliable income stream.

Your commitment to consistency creates a sense of discipline and professionalism in your business. It demonstrates your dedication to delivering high-quality service and maintaining a strong work ethic. Clients will appreciate your relatability and reliability, which will further enhance your reputation and attract more business opportunities.

Ultimately, the level of consistency you achieve in your business will contribute to long-term success and stability. By implementing your chosen pillars, delivering value to your clients, and staying top of mind, you create a strong foundation for a thriving business. As you continue to nurture and grow your client relationships, your business will naturally become more predictable, which will lead to steady income and greater financial stability.

So, stay committed to your chosen pillars, continuously refine your strategies, and embrace the mindset of delivering value and exceptional service. With time, you will see the fruits of your efforts as your business flourishes with consistent performance, increased sales, and a stable income stream.

The success of your business depends on a well-structured business and marketing plan. These plans provide a clear roadmap and serve as a guide to making sure you engage with your target audience, refine your strategies, and adapt to the evolving needs of your market. By incorporating recurring tasks into your plan, you enhance efficiency and minimize the likelihood of neglecting crucial aspects of your business.

One of the key benefits of recurring tasks is that they establish a routine and help you keep up with your marketing efforts. By setting aside dedicated time each week for tasks such as content creation, social media engagement, and customer outreach, you ensure that you are always present and active in the marketplace.

Recurring tasks also provide an opportunity to track your progress and measure the effectiveness of your marketing initiatives. By reviewing performance metrics regularly, such as website analytics, social media engagement metrics, and lead generation data, you gain insights into what is working well and what areas may need improvement. This allows you to make data-driven decisions and adjust your strategies to maximize your return on investment.

A well-structured plan is not set in stone. It is meant to be flexible and adaptable as you learn, grow, and evolve in your career. Continually assess the effectiveness of your recurring tasks, make adjustments where necessary, and seize opportunities for innovation. By doing so, you will position yourself for long-term success in the dynamic and ever-changing real estate industry.

The saying "Jack of all trades, master of none" is a commonly used expression to describe people who dabble in numerous skills without truly mastering any of them. This concept applies to choosing multiple marketing strategies as well. Rather than spreading yourself thin and delivering suboptimal results from trying to do five things ineffectively, it is better to select three pillars that align with your values and allow you expand your business over time.

Fear may always be present, but it does not have to control your actions or hinder your progress. By committing to your pillars of business, which encompass your core principles and strategies, you establish a solid foundation for growth and success.

CHAPTER NINE
*How Do You Get Your Value Proposition
Out to Build a Stable Business?*

*"A well-structured plan is not set in stone.
It is meant to be flexible and adaptable as you learn,
grow, and evolve in your real estate career."*
—Marcia Bergen

CHAPTER SUMMARY

In this chapter, I began by drawing parallels to successful personal relationships and underscored that business growth involves understanding and adapting to evolving client needs, providing personalized solutions, and building trust. I presented an array of strategies for real estate business growth, including social media use, community involvement, door knocking, cold calling, managing expired listings and for-sale-by-owner scenarios. I highlighted the role of consistency and efficient time allocation for each strategy and encouraged the use of a content calendar and regular performance analysis for continuous optimization. The principle of focusing on a few select strategies rather than scattering efforts is underlined in order to steady performance and increase sales. I explained how a systematic approach and wise time allocation, combined with consistent efforts in communication, marketing, and relationship-building, is what it takes to establish a thriving business.

REVIEW

The Three Pillars of Marketing Your Real Estate Business:
- Communication

- Planned Marketing Strategies
- Fostering Relationships

By focusing on the pillars of communication, planned marketing strategies, and fostering relationships, it is possible to overcome challenges and achieve growth.

REFLECTION QUESTIONS

1. Review your current business plan (if you have one). Considering the chapter you just read, perform an evaluation on the content and ask yourself what is working and what needs to be revisited. Make notes.
2. What are some of the challenges you foresee in door knocking and cold calling, and how can you prepare for them?
3. Can you identify the small gestures and considerations you offer your clients? If you are just starting out, consider what you offer your friends, loved ones, and community, and how you can transfer this over to client relations.
4. How do you currently allocate time for working on your business? What strategies did you learn in this chapter that you would like to incorporate?

SCENARIOS

Scenario 1: You've been spreading yourself too thin across multiple strategies, and it's affecting your productivity. What steps can you take to streamline your processes and focus your efforts?

Scenario 2: You've chosen to focus on social media marketing, community highlights, and cold calling. You've allocated time in your weekly schedule for these activities and are now seeing increased engagement on your platforms; however, you're not seeing a significant increase in leads or conversions. What would you do to turn engagement into conversions?

TO-DO LIST

- Identify three main marketing strategies you want to focus on.
- Break each strategy into tasks.
- Create a schedule that allocates each task to a weekly, monthly, and/or annual task list.
- Develop a content calendar for your newsletters, blog posts, and/or social media posts (you may have already completed this in Chapter 5).
- Set up a system for monitoring and analyzing the performance of your marketing efforts.
- If you want to move away from spreadsheets, research different online tools that can help you organize your tasks. Look into automating the scheduling and posting of your content to social media platforms.

STEP-BY-STEP INSTRUCTIONS

1. Read through the chapter and make note of the various growth strategies presented.
2. Reflect on what you've read by working through the reflection questions and scenarios.
3. Complete the tasks on your to-do list.
4. Review your goals; how do your growth strategies align?
5. Research and learn how to use available social media and internet analytics tools to monitor your website, blog, and social media engagement and conversions.

TIPS AND TAKEAWAYS

- Remember the 80/20 rule when creating social media content: 80 percent related to real estate, market conditions, and homeowner tips, and 20 percent related to your defined business personal life.
- Understand the nuances of each social media platform and tailor your content accordingly.
- Regularly track and analyze the performance of your marketing efforts.

- Community connections can help you enhance your reach and credibility.
- Regularly track and analyze the performance of your marketing efforts.
- Stay focused on your chosen marketing strategies rather than spreading yourself too thin.

Your own takeaways:

- _____
  _____
- _____
  _____
- _____
  _____

"There is nothing like a concrete life plan to weigh you down. Because if you always have one eye on some future goal, you stop paying attention to the job at hand, miss opportunities that might arise, and stay fixedly on one path, even when a better, newer course might have opened up."
—Indra K. Nooyi, CEO of Pepsi Co.

CHAPTER TEN
Get Down to Business

"A good system shortens the road to the goal."
—Orison Swett Marden

In previous chapters we discussed the importance of establishing your core values and the details of building a marketing plan based on the credentials you identified. Within the real estate industry, some essential aspects form the backbone of a business, even though they may not be directly visible to clients. These behind-the-scenes operations ensure the smooth functioning and long-term success of our business ventures.

When you are developing your business and systems, understand that the small things become the big things over time. You are laying the groundwork on the assumption that your business will grow beyond your current expectations. This can be likened to birthing a baby and investing money into a Registered Education Savings Plan each month. You are doing this on the assumption of greater aspirations for your child. Your child is a simile to your business.

In this chapter you, will come to recognize the power of optimizing efficiency within your expenses, business planning, and client management. Additionally, you will gain a deeper understanding of the importance of tracking your clients to foster continuous expansion rather than constantly reinventing your client base and overall business strategy.

Efficiency, expense, and client tracking are essential for a successful real estate business. These principles become evident when considering the four main categories required to operate and grow a business: accounting, business planning, database management, and efficiencies through creating precedent.

Accounting serves as the financial backbone of our business. It involves managing the financial transactions, recording and tracking expenses and revenues, and ensuring compliance with tax laws and regulations. Effective accounting practices enable us to monitor our cash flow, analyze profitability, and make informed financial decisions. By maintaining accurate records and financial statements, we can assess the health of our business and identify areas for improvement or growth. Proper accounting practices help establish credibility with lenders, investors, and other stakeholders who may require financial information before entering into business partnerships or transactions. While accounting may not be directly visible to clients, it plays a role in maintaining the financial stability and sustainability of our business.

The financial health and success of your business depends on you knowing how to organize and manage your accounting. Allocating time on a monthly basis to input your expenses by category or hiring a bookkeeper (if your budget allows) can save time when it comes to tax season. My tax deadline often coincides with one of the busiest times of real estate transactions; therefore, being prepared in advance ensures that I will not end up in a situation where I cannot organize my income and expense while doing my best to serve my clients.

Drawing from my experiences in managing a small law firm and a property development business, I have implemented a system of categorizing my expenses in accounting software. This approach helps me stay organized and on track with the budget I set at the beginning of each year for marketing, charitable support, and personal expenses. By maintaining clear categories for expenses, I can easily track and analyze my financial data.

When organizing your expenses, consider these key categories:

Broker Expenses: This includes your monthly dues to the broker and any reductions made from your commission based on the split you negotiated. Keep track of these expenses so you can understand your financial obligations to the brokerage and maintain transparency in your financial dealings.

Rent or Office Expenses: If you have a stand-alone office, you should include the costs associated with rent, internet services, utilities, and maintenance. Properly track these expenses to assess the financial impact of your office space and make informed decisions regarding its sustainability.

Office Supplies and Materials: This category covers expenses related to office supplies, marketing materials, and print marketing costs. Track these expenses to manage your inventory, control costs, and ensure you have the necessary materials to effectively run your business.

Marketing Costs: Marketing is a critical component of your business. Include expenses for advertising, promotional gifts, client gifts, and any other marketing initiatives you undertake. By tracking these costs, you can evaluate the effectiveness of your marketing strategies and allocate resources to the most impactful channels.

Charitable Donations: Many real estate professionals support local or global organizations through charitable donations. Track these contributions, as they reflect your personal values and have financial implications for your business. Keep a record of your charitable donations to stay aligned with your philanthropic goals and manage your overall budget.

Vehicle Expenses: If you use a vehicle for business purposes, track related expenses such as fuel, lease costs, maintenance, and insurance. These costs can have a significant impact on your bottom line, and accurately monitoring them allows you to assess the financial implications of using a vehicle for your real estate activities.

Social Costs: Networking and relationship-building are integral parts of growing your business. This category includes expenses related to business lunches, sponsorship costs, and any other expenditures incurred when connecting with clients and industry professionals. By tracking these costs, you can evaluate the return on investment from networking activities and adjust your approach accordingly.

These examples represent just a fraction of the possible expense categories you might encounter in your real estate business. Consult with your personal accountant and bookkeeper to ensure you are accurately tracking and organizing your expenses. By providing efficient and accurate financial information, you can minimize costs and streamline your accounting processes.

Maintaining a well-organized accounting system not only helps you meet your financial obligations, but also provides insights into the financial health of your business. By regularly reviewing your expenses and financial statements, you can identify areas for improvement, make informed decisions, and ensure the long-term success and stability of your real estate venture.

Budgeting is an integral part of business planning, as your financial situation dictates the execution of your marketing and client retention plan. By developing a financial plan, you can effectively allocate resources, monitor expenses, and ensure the financial health of your business. This includes projecting revenues, estimating costs, and identifying potential areas for cost savings or investment.

Budgeting involves carefully allocating your financial resources to maximize the effectiveness of your investments and ensure the growth and sustainability of your business. By creating a well-structured budget, you can will see where your efforts and money are best spent, which allows you to make informed decisions and plan for future success.

Budgeting allows you to track and monitor your expenses, income, and overall financial health. It involves categorizing your expenses, such as broker fees, office rent, marketing costs, and other operational expenses. Allocating a specific budget for each category ensures that your financial resources are properly managed and that you have a clear overview of your cash flow. This helps you identify areas where you can reduce costs, optimize spending, and increase profitability. By having a solid grasp of your financial situation, you can make informed decisions about pricing, investments, and other financial aspects of your business.

It is apparent why budgeting is a vital component of effective business planning. It allows you to allocate resources strategically and set realistic goals and targets for your business. By analyzing market trends, competitor activities, and internal capabilities, you can determine the areas where your investments will yield the highest returns. This may include marketing campaigns, training and development programs, technology upgrades, or expanding your team. By setting a budget for these activities, you will likely have enough money to execute your plans and achieve your desired outcomes.

Budgeting also provides a sense of control and discipline in your business operations. It helps you prioritize your expenses and avoid unnecessary or impulsive spending. By carefully considering your financial resources and aligning them with your business goals, you can make strategic choices that drive growth and profitability. Budgeting enables you to anticipate and mitigate financial risks and also ensures that you have sufficient reserves and contingency plans in place.

Creating a budget requires careful analysis and planning. Start by evaluating your historical financial data and identifying patterns and trends. Consider your business goals and the strategies you intend to implement to achieve them. This will help you determine the financial resources needed to support your initiatives. Regularly review and update your budget as market conditions and business circumstances change. This allows you to adapt your financial plans and reallocate resources as necessary.

Budgeting software or spreadsheets can be valuable tools for managing your budget. They provide a structured framework for organizing and tracking your financial data so you can monitor your income and expenses, track variances, and make adjustments as needed. Set aside some time each year to consult with an accountant or financial advisor for help with developing and managing your budget.

By creating a well-structured budget, you will see where you are spending your efforts and money. This perspective helps you to optimize your investments and drives long-term success. Embracing budgeting as a core business practice will help you navigate the financial landscape with confidence and achieve your goals. By revisiting the adage that a dollar saved is a dollar earned, it becomes evident that monitoring costs is an efficient way to ensure your efforts yield the most profit.

While our clients may not directly witness our business planning efforts, those efforts are the foundation that guides our daily operations and drives our success. This foundation enables us to adapt to changes in the market, make informed decisions, and allocate resources. By regularly reviewing and updating our business plan, we can stay agile and responsive to market dynamics.

I conduct an annual audit to assess where my business has grown. This involves tracking where my clients came from and identifying the referral sources that resulted from the strategic plans I executed in the previous year. This analysis allows me to identify the most effective marketing and lead generation strategies and refine my approach for future growth.

Business planning also provides the ability to adapt to market changes. By staying informed about industry trends and shifts in customer preferences, we can adjust our strategies and tactics accordingly. This flexibility allows us to stay ahead of the competition and better serve our clients.

Outside of the budget business planning is a fundamental aspect of running a successful real estate business. It involves conducting market research, defining target markets, setting business goals, budgeting, and risk management. Although clients may not witness these efforts directly, they form the foundation that drives our business operations and enables us to achieve long-term success. By engaging in strategic business planning, we can adapt to market changes, make informed decisions, and allocate resources to position ourselves competitively within the industry.

The creation and management of a client database is one of the most valuable assets you can develop. Studies have shown that when you have a database of around 250 contacts, you can expect to generate approximately $1 million to $2 million in gross commission annually, depending on your market and the average sale price in your area. This figure includes both past and current clients, as well as strong referral sources who consistently send you business.

I didn't start keeping track of my clients in a formal database until my third year in the business. The difference between my second and third year was remarkable, as my gross commission doubled. This significant improvement can be attributed to implementing a system that allowed me to track and engage with my clients and referral sources in a consistent and planned manner. Despite the minimal expense involved, having a focused and direct plan of communicating with clients made a world of difference.

Database management maintains and leverages client relationships and information. Using a database organizes and stores client data, including contact details, transaction history, preferences, and other pertinent information. This enables us to streamline communication, provide personalized services, and cultivate long-term client relationships. By segmenting our database and using customer relationship management tools, we can tailor our marketing efforts and deliver targeted messages to specific client segments. This ensures that we stay top-of-mind with our clients and offer them relevant and timely information while anticipating their needs.

A well-maintained database facilitates lead generation, tracking, and conversion, which enhances the ability to generate new business opportunities. When used effectively, your database ensures that potential clients do not fall through the cracks. By leveraging your database, you can engage with leads in a timely manner and guide them through the buying or selling process.

The ability to maintain accurate records, engage in targeted communication, and anticipate clients' needs is greatly enhanced by database management. It provides a level of service that goes beyond expectations and ensures that our clients become enthusiastic advocates for our business.

A well-managed client database significantly contributes to the success of your business. By leveraging the power of database management, you optimize your communication, nurture client relationships, generate new business opportunities, and deliver exceptional experiences. It is an investment that yields substantial returns and sets the foundation for long-term growth and success in the industry.

To ensure the effectiveness of these behind-the-scenes operations, adhere to the following principles:

Accuracy and Compliance: Upholding accuracy in financial records, adhering to accounting standards, and complying with legal and regulatory requirements maintain the integrity of financial operations. This includes accurately recording transactions, filing taxes on time, and keeping up with any changes in accounting regulations. Based on where your business is located, you may also be governed by legislation that requires you to keep all client communication, forms, or data for a specified period of time. Review these retention requirements with your broker to ensure you are tracking and storing the necessary information.

Proactive Planning: Engage in proactive business planning to anticipate challenges, capitalize on opportunities, and set realistic goals. By regularly reviewing and updating your business plans, you adapt to market conditions and steer your business in the right direction.

Data Integrity and Security: Maintaining the integrity and security of your database protects client information and ensures compliance with data protection regulations. Implementing robust data management practices, using secure storage systems, and safeguarding client confidentiality is paramount.

Continual Learning and Improvement: To stay ahead in the ever-evolving real estate industry, embrace a mindset of continual learning and improvement. Keep up with market trends, attend industry conferences, participate in professional development opportunities, and seek feedback from clients.

After establishing the framework for the three essential categories of accounting and budgeting, business planning, and client database management, the next step in creating efficiencies within your business is to establish precedents for repetitive activities. You achieve this by creating templates for commonly used forms such as an offer to purchase, listing contracts, service agreements, and condition-removal documents. You will save time by prefilling these templates with static information like your name, contact details, and brokerage information. While it may seem insignificant to save a few minutes each time, the cumulative effect becomes apparent when you find yourself saving several minutes multiple times a day.

In addition to creating document templates, develop a comprehensive manual that outlines the step-by-step processes involved in the tasks associated with running your business. This manual will also serve as a valuable resource for any future assistants or employees you may bring on board. It provides a clear guide for understanding how you personally plan and operate your business so you can delegate certain operations.

For example, when inputting a listing, you can create a detailed step-by-step guide that outlines the necessary actions from gathering property information to preparing marketing materials. Similarly, developing buyer and seller checklists ensures that all steps are followed throughout the transaction process, regardless of who is managing the tasks. By establishing and adhering to these checklists, you maintain the quality and professionalism of your business, even if responsibilities are delegated to a new employee.

The early stages of building a business can be exhilarating, but the personal satisfaction derived from conducting real estate transactions can be rewarding. To reap those rewards, lay a solid foundation by creating processes and templates. These tools leverage your time and enable you to scale and expand your business without sacrificing quality or consistency.

By implementing these strategies, you streamline your operations, reduce the likelihood of errors or oversights, and create a more productive and sustainable business. Moreover, the development of standardized processes and templates sets the stage for future growth and makes it easier to onboard new team members or expand your business offerings.

Creating efficiencies is an ongoing process. Continuously evaluate and refine your processes and templates as your business evolves and new opportunities arise. Stay open to feedback and suggestions from your team members or employees, as they may see where further streamlining is possible.

By establishing precedents through templates, checklists, and comprehensive manuals, you create efficiencies within your business that save time, ensure consistency, and set the stage for future growth. Investing the time and effort to develop these tools will enable you to leverage your resources, maximize productivity, and position your business for long-term success while minimizing the effort and mental stress during times that your business is seeing growth.

CHAPTER TEN
Get Down to Business

*"In the world of real estate, the most successful
agent is the most adaptable."*
—Anonymous

CHAPTER SUMMARY

In this chapter, I underscored the role of efficient expense tracking, strategic business planning, and robust client management in bolstering the success of a real estate business. The key to financial stability is maintaining a structured accounting system and a well-orchestrated budget, with categorized expenses such as broker charges, rent, marketing, donations, vehicle-related outlays, and social costs. I emphasized the necessity of formulating and periodically revising a budget that aligns with business objectives and market trends, ensuring strategic resource allocation and financial risk mitigation. Furthermore, I shed light on the importance of business planning, allowing adaptability in the face of market changes, informed decision-making, and effective resource management. I delved into the significance of database management, particularly of a client database, as a tool for improved communication, relationship nurturing, and new business generation. Finally, I highlighted the need for creating efficient processes and templates for recurring activities, promoting consistency, productivity, and fostering long-term business growth.

REVIEW

Main Categories for the Operation and Growth of a Business:

Accounting and Budgeting

- Bookkeeping
- Record and track expenses and revenues
- Ensure compliance with tax laws and regulations
- Maintain accurate records and financial statements
- Develop a financial plan

Business Planning

- Conduct market research
- Define target markets
- Set business goals
- Establish a budget
- Risk management

CHAPTER SUMMARY

In this chapter, I underscored the role of efficient expense track-ing, strategic business planning, and robust client management in bolstering the success of a real estate business. The key to financial stability is maintaining a structured accounting sys-tem and a well-orchestrated budget, with categorized expenses such as broker charges, rent, marketing, donations, vehicle-related outlays, and social costs. I emphasized the necessity of formulating and periodically revising a budget that aligns with business objectives and market trends, ensuring strategic resource allocation and financial risk mitigation. Furthermore, I shed light on the importance of business planning, allowing adaptability in the face of market changes, informed decision-making, and effective resource management. I delved into the significance of database management, particularly of a client database, as a tool for improved communication, relationship nurturing, and new business generation. Finally, I highlighted the need for creating efficient processes and templates for recurring activities, promoting consistency, productivity, and fostering long-term business growth.

REVIEW

Main Categories for the Operation and Growth of a Business:

Accounting and Budgeting

- Bookkeeping
- Record and track expenses and revenues
- Ensure compliance with tax laws and regulations
- Maintain accurate records and financial statements
- Develop a financial plan

Business Planning

- Conduct market research
- Define target markets
- Set business goals
- Establish a budget
- Risk management
- Regular business auditing and analysis

Database Management

- Track and engage with clients and referral sources
- Maintain and leverage client relationships and information
- Organize and store client data
- Facilitate lead generation, tracking, and conversion

Creating Efficient Processes

- Create templates for commonly used forms
- Develop comprehensive manuals that outline step-by-step processes used to run your business
- Create checklists, such as buyer and seller checklists to follow throughout the transaction process

REFLECTION QUESTIONS

1. How are you currently tracking your business expenses and budget? Is this method effective?
2. Is your business currently set up to adapt to changes in the market and customer preferences?

3. How do you currently manage your client information and data? Based on what you've read, is your current model effective? Or, if you are starting out, how do you plan to manage client data?

SCENARIOS

Scenario 1: You are a real estate agent just starting a new business. You need to establish what your baseline monthly income should be in order to keep your operations going while you get your business going. What steps do you need to take to figure this out?

Scenario 2: You are an established real estate agent who has been maintaining their files, finances, and client databases on spreadsheets, and you want to streamline your operations. After conducting an annual audit, you identify the need to introduce tools or software to create efficiencies in your business. What types of tools and software would you choose?

TO-DO LIST

- Review the "Main Categories for the Operation and Growth of a Business" under the Review section.
- Check the items off that you feel confident and prepared to move forward with. Plan to address the remaining unchecked items.
- Continue to audit your existing business plan (if applicable) and see what you need to incorporate or adjust based on what you've learned in this chapter.
- Research CRM software for client data management. Ask other realtors what they use. Determine your business needs and compare them to the CRM features. Compare price points. Assess which one would meet your budget and needs. If you're not ready for CRM, explore spreadsheet templates that suit your needs.
- Explore and implement budgeting software or tools if you aren't already.

STEP-BY-STEP INSTRUCTIONS

1. Read through the chapter and make note of the growth strategies presented.
2. Reflect on what you've read by working through the reflection questions and scenarios.
3. Complete the tasks on your to-do list.
4. Review your goals; think about how the tools you read about in this chapter will help you attain them.

TIPS AND TAKEAWAYS

- Regularly review and update your business plan to ensure agility and responsiveness.
- Keep a close eye on industry trends to adapt your business strategies accordingly.
- Use a client database to streamline communication and provide personalized services.
- Strictly adhere to legal and regulatory requirements to maintain the integrity of your business.
- Keep a clear record of all transactions for future reference and tax purposes.
- Regularly review your budget to make necessary adjustments based on market trends and business performance.
- Consult with an accountant or financial advisor to ensure accurate and efficient financial management.

Your own takeaways:

- _____
  _____
- _____
  _____
- _____
  _____

CHAPTER ELEVEN
Nurturing Clients and Referral Sources

> *"Acknowledging the good that is already in your life is the foundation for all abundance."*
> **—Eckhart Tolle**

As we delve into the organization and structure of your business, you will come to understand the significance of nurturing your past clients and referral sources. Nurturing behaviors generate recurring business while strengthening and diversifying your referral network.

To begin, revisit your core values and the vision you have for your business. These foundational elements will guide the development of your follow-up and client retention plan. Aligning your actions with your values fosters long-term relationships and establishes a solid foundation for the growth and sustainability of your business.

Neglecting to nurture this aspect of your business can result in a continuous cycle of having to reinvent your business. In a previous chapter, I emphasized the importance of *tracking* your clients and referral sources using a database. It is equally important to have a plan for *engaging* with the clients in your database.

This strategy serves as a cornerstone for the longevity of your business. By implementing effective client retention strategies, you solidify your relationships and increase the likelihood of repeat business and referrals.

Here are some key approaches to consider:

Personalized Communication: Regularly reach out to your clients through personalized and meaningful communication. This can include sending holiday greetings, birthday acknowledgments, personalized thank-you notes with gift cards to local restaurants, or monthly updates on the real estate market. Showing genuine interest in clients' lives and demonstrating your commitment to their success will strengthen the bond between you. A business plan that includes 12 to 14 personal touches for each individual in your database can yield continued business and referrals that increase your business by up to 30 percent each year.

Stay Top of Mind: Implement strategies to remain top of mind with your clients. This can be achieved through monthly newsletters, informative blog posts, or social media engagement. By providing relevant content, you position yourself as a trusted resource and expert in your field.

Offer Continued Support: Do not limit your interaction with clients to the transactional aspect of real estate. Offer ongoing support and guidance by providing home maintenance tips, information about local community events, or referrals to trusted professionals in related industries. By demonstrating your commitment to their overall well-being, you solidify your position as their go-to real estate advisor.

Client Appreciation Events: Organize client appreciation events to show your gratitude and strengthen relationships. These events can range from small gatherings, such as brunch or happy hour, to larger events like annual client parties. By creating opportunities for face-to-face interactions, you foster a sense of connection and reinforce how much you value your clients.

Referral Programs: Implement referral programs to encourage clients and referral sources to recommend your services.

This can involve exclusive benefits for referrals that result in closed transactions. By acknowledging and rewarding their support, you encourage them to continue referring business to you. You must be mindful of the legislation governing the rules of your real estate association, as some do not allow the payment of referrals or monetary reward for referrals.

By implementing these strategies and nurturing your past clients and referral sources, you establish a foundation for the long-term success and growth of your business. Maintaining and expanding your existing network is often more cost-effective and yields higher-quality leads than solely relying on new lead generation efforts.

Nurturing your past clients and referral sources is one of the most important strategies of all, as it will cement the longevity of your business. By aligning your actions with your core values, personalized communication, staying top of mind, offering continued support, organizing client appreciation events, and implementing referral programs, you cultivate lasting relationships, secure repeat business, and strengthen your referral network.

Ensuring client satisfaction and cultivating strong referral sources are integral to the success and growth of your business. Happy clients not only lead to repeat business but also become your advocates when they refer you to their friends, family, and colleagues. Building and maintaining these relationships requires dedicated effort and a customer-centric approach.

Be mindful of the key components covered in previous chapters when developing your strategy for generating repeat business and keeping your referral resources strong. Here are some key strategies to remember:

Provide Exceptional Customer Service: Going above and beyond to deliver outstanding customer service should be at the forefront of your business. Be responsive, attentive, and proactive in addressing your clients' needs and concerns. Promptly return calls and emails, provide regular updates, and actively listen to their preferences and feedback.

Build Strong Personal Connections: Real estate is a people-centric industry, and building personal connections is essential. Take the time to get to know your clients on a deeper level. Understand their goals, interests, and preferences. Show genuine care and empathy, and go the extra mile to make them feel valued and understood. Remember important details about their lives, send personalized messages or gifts on special occasions, and maintain regular communication even after the transaction is complete.

Communicate Effectively and Transparently: Open and transparent communication maintains trust and satisfaction. Keep your clients informed about every step of the process. Explain complex concepts in a clear and understandable manner. Set realistic expectations and proactively manage any potential challenges. Regularly update your clients on the progress of their transaction, even if there are no major developments. Communication builds confidence and helps alleviate any concerns or uncertainties.

Provide Value Beyond the Transaction: To create long-term relationships with your clients, offer value beyond the immediate transaction. Share market insights, provide tips on home maintenance and improvement, and connect them with reputable service providers in your network.

Ask for Feedback and Act on it: Actively seek feedback from your clients to gauge their level of satisfaction and identify areas for improvement. Send surveys or schedule follow-up meetings to discuss their experience working with you. Take their feedback seriously and make necessary adjustments to enhance your service. Clients appreciate being heard, and their feedback can guide your continuous growth and improvement.

Cultivate Referral Sources: Referral sources are a valuable asset that help grow your business. Develop and maintain strong relationships with past clients, fellow professionals, and community influencers who can refer potential clients to you. Stay connected with them through regular touchpoints such as newsletters, personalized emails, or social media interactions. Acknowledge and show appreciation for their support by expressing gratitude and recognizing their contributions to your success.

Provide Incentives for Referrals: Encourage referrals by implementing a referral program that rewards both the referring party and the new client. Offer incentives such as discounts on future services, gift cards, or exclusive access to special events or resources. This not only motivates clients to make referrals but also reinforces your commitment to building lasting relationships and providing exceptional value.

Continuously Invest in Professional Development: To stay at the top of your game and provide exceptional service, invest in continuous professional development. Stay updated on market trends, industry best practices, and emerging technologies. Attend conferences, workshops, and training sessions to enhance your knowledge and skills. The more expertise you can offer, the more confident your clients and referral sources will be in recommending your services.

By focusing on client satisfaction and nurturing strong referral sources, you can build a thriving real estate business. The key is to prioritize exceptional customer service, build personal connections, communicate regularly, provide ongoing value, seek feedback, and cultivate a network of advocates. Happy clients and strong referral sources are the foundation of your long-term success. You do not want to re-establish your business year after year, so keep your existing clients happy and happy to refer business to you.

During the early stages of my career, I embraced the philosophy of maintaining regular contact with clients and referral sources through a strategy of monthly touches or communication using my database. This approach allowed me to stay connected and top of mind so I could nurture relationships and foster a sense of loyalty.

Here are the specific methods I employed to achieve this:

Monthly Newsletter: Mailing a newsletter each month proved to be an effective way of providing my clients and referral sources with information and updates. This tangible and personalized communication showcased my expertise, shared market insights, and included personal touches such as local recommendations or home maintenance tips. The consistency of this monthly touchpoint reinforced my commitment to staying connected and keeping them informed.

Bimonthly Blogging: Leveraging the power of digital platforms, I published blog posts on my website twice a month. These blog articles served as an additional channel to provide content and establish myself as an industry thought leader. By addressing common questions, discussing market trends, and sharing helpful tips, I aimed to position myself as a reliable resource for my audience. Regularly updating my blog showcased my expertise and drove traffic to my website and increased my online visibility.

Quarterly Client Calls: Making quarterly calls to my clients allowed me to check in, maintain rapport, and address any questions or concerns they had. These calls were not focused solely on business matters but also provided an opportunity for personal conversation and relationship-building. By showing genuine interest and taking the time to listen, I strengthened my connections and reinforced the trust and loyalty my clients had in me. These calls also served as a reminder that I was available and dedicated to serving their real estate needs.

Biannual Client Events: Hosting two client events per year was an effective way to express gratitude and show appreciation for their continued support. These events ranged from casual gatherings, such as a summer barbecue or holiday party, to more formal occasions like a client appreciation dinner. These events provided an opportunity to connect face-to-face, foster a sense of community among my clients, and deepen the relationships I had built. They also served as a platform for clients to network and refer potential business to me.

By implementing these strategies, I was able to engage with my clients and referral sources to reinforce the value I provided and solidify my position as their trusted real estate professional. The combination of a monthly newsletter, bimonthly blogging, quarterly client calls, and biannual client events created a well-rounded and comprehensive approach to maintaining regular contact throughout the year.

While these specific tactics worked well for me, each real estate professional has their own unique mix of touchpoints that align with their business style and target audience. The key is to find a balance between personalization and value creation in order to keep clients satisfied and referral sources strong. By prioritizing regular and meaningful interactions, you can nurture lasting relationships that contribute to the growth and success of your business.

Real estate agents must understand the value of each client and the potential for future business through referrals. It can be challenging for new agents to grasp the long-term impact of providing exceptional service and exceeding industry standards. By going above and beyond, agents can retain clients for future transactions and unlock the potential for organic lead generation through direct referrals.

Referrals are often considered "soft leads" because they come from someone who has had a positive experience working with an agent. These leads have a higher conversion rate compared to cold leads, as a level of trust and familiarity already exists; therefore, agents must prioritize delivering exceptional service to ensure client satisfaction and increase the likelihood of receiving referrals.

For agents with limited budgets or a preference for face-to-face interactions, focusing on soft leads can be a comfortable and effective approach. Building relationships through open houses, networking events, or connections with past clients allows for personal introductions and a higher level of trust from the outset. Clients who have witnessed an agent's marketing strategies and results are more likely to create a continuous stream of potential business by referring their own contacts to the agent.

Relying solely on mass lead generation or paid leads do not necessarily lead to long-term success. While these methods can generate initial leads, they may not have the same level of trust or connection as referrals from satisfied clients. Building a business based on organic referrals establishes a solid foundation of trust and credibility, which can lead to a sustainable and growing client base.

As an introverted agent, I understand the importance of leveraging personal connections and focusing on soft leads. By providing exceptional service and delivering results, I have been able to cultivate strong relationships and receive a steady stream of referrals. This approach has allowed me to build my business without relying heavily on paid leads or mass marketing efforts.

Real estate agents must maintain a strong and ongoing relationship with clients beyond the closing of a deal. Avoid the perception of being solely driven by financial gain and instead focus on providing value and building meaningful connections. Neglecting to follow up and engage with clients after a transaction can be seen as a lack of genuine interest in their well-being and may damage the agent's reputation.

Building a sense of connection and fostering long-term relationships with clients is key. Using clients' names, asking about their lives, and showing genuine care and interest are essential elements of successful client management. People appreciate agents who take the time to understand their needs, preferences, and goals. Avoiding the stereotype of a pushy salesperson who only promotes themselves and their services is vital to building trust and rapport.

Engage with clients on topics beyond their immediate real estate needs. Sharing information about appealing tax strategies, discussing renovation ideas and costs, or providing updates on current market valuations and financing options demonstrates the agent's expertise and commitment to supporting clients in all aspects of their homeownership journey. By offering ongoing support and being responsive to past clients' needs, agents lay the foundation for continued conversations and strengthen their relationship over time.

The conversation with clients should not end with the closing of a deal. Real estate agents should strive to go beyond the transactional aspect and build lasting relationships based on trust, care, and ongoing support. By continually providing value and staying connected, agents cultivate a strong sense of connection and build a network of satisfied clients who are more likely to recommend an agent's services and continue working with them in the future.

Creating a business built on the philosophy of giving is a powerful approach that sets the stage for establishing strong relationships and garnering trust from your clients. When you operate your business with the intention of providing value and genuine concern for their financial and real estate needs, people come to rely on you as a trusted advisor and advocate.

By adopting a giving mindset, you prioritize the needs and interests of your clients above your own. This approach fosters a sense of reciprocity and positions you as someone who genuinely cares about their well-being. Instead of solely focusing on transactions and immediate gains, concentrate on building long-term relationships based on trust and mutual benefit.

The philosophy of giving is not a one-time action but rather a mindset and approach that should permeate all aspects of your business. By demonstrating your dedication to giving, you create a virtuous cycle of trust, referrals, and long-term success.

CHAPTER ELEVEN
Nurturing Clients and Referral Services

*"A happy client not only leads to repeat business,
but also to becoming your advocate."*
—**Marcia Bergen**

CHAPTER SUMMARY

In this chapter, I emphasize the importance of nurturing past clients and referral sources as a cornerstone for a successful real estate business. I advocate for aligning core values and vision with a robust follow-up and client retention plan, detailing four key methods I use: monthly newsletters, bimonthly blogging, quarterly client calls, and biannual client events. To emphasize the importance of referrals, I underline the need to exceed customer expectations and offer continued support to obtain these referrals. I also underscore the significance of maintaining connections beyond the immediate transaction and organizing client appreciation events to foster this relationship. My strategy also includes cultivating referral sources and proactively seeking opportunities for professional development. Central to my philosophy is a focus on the clients' needs. Advocating for a philosophy of giving forms the backbone of my business approach.

REVIEW

Key approaches to nurturing clients and referral sources:
- Personalize communication
- Stay top of mind

- Offer continued support
- Host client appreciation events
- Cultivate referral sources through programs and incentives
- Provide exceptional customer service
- Build strong personal connections
- Communicate effectively and transparently
- Provide value beyond the transaction
- Ask for feedback and act on it
- Invest in professional development

REFLECTION QUESTIONS

1. What is the role of referrals in the real estate business?
2. Why is the philosophy of giving significant in the real estate business?
3. What strategies can you implement to improve personalized communication and stay top of mind with clients?
4. What activities do you use, or will you consider using, to foster strong personal connections?

SCENARIOS

Scenario 1: Six months after closing a transaction with a client, you realize that you have neither reached out to nor heard from them. What steps can you take to re-engage them and strengthen the relationship?

Scenario 2: You have a limited budget and are looking for ways to generate leads. What strategies and methods will you implement to nurture clients and referrals without incurring extra costs?

TO-DO LIST

- Review your core values and mission statement for your business from Chapter 3.

- Develop a client retention plan that aligns with your values and mission by using the tools and strategies learned in this chapter as a guide.
- Develop a referral program.
- Develop or audit your strategy for regular client communication: newsletters, blogs, calls, or events (you may have done this in Chapter 5).

STEP-BY-STEP INSTRUCTIONS

1. Read the chapter and note the items you would like to incorporate into your business.
2. Complete the reflection questions and scenarios.
3. Work through the to-do list.
4. Review your goals, core values, and vision. Do they align?
5. Review the tools and strategies from previous chapters and continue to synthesize what you are learning into a cohesive plan for your business.

TIPS AND TAKEAWAYS

- Maintain regular, meaningful communication with your clients and referral sources.
- Do not limit your interaction to transactional aspects. Offer value beyond this by sharing resources and knowledge.
- Actively seek feedback from your clients and make necessary adjustments.
- Regularly invest in professional development to stay updated and provide the best service.
- Communicate regularly with clients to foster a sense of loyalty and stay top of mind.
- Deliver exceptional service to help generate referrals, which have a higher conversion rate than cold leads.
- Maintain relationships beyond the transaction phase to help reinforce trust and generate repeat business.

- Adopt a philosophy of giving to foster a sense of reciprocity and position you as a trusted advisor in your clients' eyes.

Your own takeaways:

- _____
  _____
- _____
  _____
- _____
  _____

CHAPTER TWELVE
Sex and Real Estate

"Strong women wear their pain like stilettos.
No matter how much it hurts, all you
see is the beauty of it."
—Harriet Morgan

If someone had told me that, at fifty years old, I would find myself compromising my safety during work relations, I would never have believed it.

The real estate industry exposes individuals, particularly women, to various situations where they may encounter unwelcome advances and place themselves in compromising positions.

In January of 2022, I agreed to meet a former colleague who needed advice on color and flooring to enhance the resale value of his condo. Little did I know that this encounter would result in an assault. I was forcefully pushed into a bathroom, my body partially exposed, and I was held against my will. Fear consumed me. With the support of my family and closest friends, I mustered the courage to report the incident to the police. Recounting the story was both terrifying and degrading, as it carried an overwhelming sense of shame.

Through this process, it became evident that none of the governing associations in my jurisdiction had any protocols or policies in place to address instances of assault, regardless of the nature. It was 2022, and yet there were no measures to protect the well-being of their members or the general public. Determined to bring about change, I took it upon myself to initiate this necessary transformation; however, it remains an ongoing endeavor.

Approximately six months later, a member of my team was in the process of taking down signs and advertisements at an open house. She was preparing to leave when two men approached her. They explained that they had intended to arrive within the advertised time frame and apologized for their tardiness. They requested a quick walk-through of the house and convinced her to unlock the door to grant them access. Once inside, one of the men locked the door behind her.

Sensing that something was wrong, she pretended to receive a call and immediately contacted me. She informed me that she was still at the open house and that two men had arrived just after it officially ended. Concerned for her safety, I asked if she was all right, to which she replied with uncertainty. I instructed her to inform the men that she had to take the call and would catch up with them shortly. As the two men left the room, I advised her to step outside the house. Following my guidance, she made her way to her vehicle and locked herself inside.

In that tense moment, I asked her to carefully document a description of the two men and their license plate. Unfortunately, the out-of-province license plate had been muddied by the mild spring weather. Nevertheless, she captured a partial plate number and noted the color and make of the vehicle. The two men, after completing their walk-through, approached her vehicle and requested that she go back inside the house to retrieve a feature listing sheet for the property. Sensibly, she refused.

After reporting this incident to the police, we were informed that the license plate on the vehicle had been stolen. Additionally, one of the men matched the description provided by a female agent in a neighboring province who had reported a similar encounter. It was only then that my team member realized the gravity of the situation and how devastating the outcome could have been.

Safety is a critical concern in any profession, but it becomes even more pronounced in an industry where professionals regularly encounter unfamiliar individuals in empty properties, such as buildings, houses, and condos. The nature of real estate, with its emphasis on advertising and establishing connections with buyers and sellers through marketing efforts, exacerbates this issue and makes it incredibly challenging to completely avoid potential risks.

I recently had the opportunity to meet with several agents in preparation for an upcoming panel discussion called "Crucial Conversations" that we would be partaking in. The panel delves into various topics with realtor safety being at the forefront.

During our discussions, I was disheartened to hear some of the comments shared by fellow agents. One agent expressed how they had encountered a listing appointment that was so alarming they felt compelled to run away, overcome by fear. Another agent confessed that they endured disrespectful and sexually demeaning language from a client to secure the business and close a deal. Additionally, it was revealed that a lot of female agents resort to having someone accompany them or wait in the car during showings. These conversations shed light on the unfortunate reality that such dialogue and situations are all too common for female agents. The safety concerns they face are undeniable and the experiences shared have reinforced the pressing need for discussions around realtor safety. It is a critical issue that requires attention and action within the industry.

If you are considering entering a one-on-one sales business that involves taking sign calls and cold leads, here are five recommendations to consider for your safety:

Request Photo Identification: Before meeting with someone, ask them to send you photo identification via text message or email. This verifies their identity and provides an additional layer of security.

Have a Safety Person on Standby: Arrange for a safety person to be available during meetings. This can involve either having someone accompany you or keeping them on an active phone line throughout the encounter.

Wear Appropriate Footwear: Opt for shoes or boots that make it easy for you to move quickly, if needed. Comfortable running shoes can make a difference in the event you find yourself in a potentially unsafe situation.

Dress Professionally: Dress in a manner that strictly conveys professionalism and leaves no room for misinterpretation. Avoid attire that may be seen as provocative or suggestive to ensure the focus remains solely on the business at hand.

Maintain Situational Awareness: Never turn your back to a stranger and always position yourself closer to the exit or door than the person you are meeting. This allows you to maintain better control of the situation and provides a means of quick escape, if necessary.

These recommendations are aimed at prioritizing your safety and minimizing potential risks when engaging in one-on-one sales interactions. Trust your instincts and take necessary precautions to protect yourself throughout the process.

Another suggestion to enhance your safety in the one-on-one sales business is to obtain a secondary phone number to list in your advertisements. If that is not feasible, use your office number instead. This approach helps separate your personal and professional communications and reduces the risk of unwanted callers disguising their intentions as property inquiries.

Be mindful of the content you share on social media platforms. Limiting or avoiding posting potentially revealing or provocative photos, such as bikini pictures, can minimize the volume of unwanted attention and contact from individuals with ill intentions. Remember, your online presence serves as a reflection of your business, so maintain a professional image and showcase content focused only on your work or family to deter unwanted interactions.

Taking measures to safeguard your social media and online presence, ensuring it predominantly consists of professional or family-oriented content, reduces the number of unwelcome individuals who reach out to you. Prioritize your safety, even if it means restricting certain aspects of your online activity.

Some men employ various tactics to isolate and connect with women, particularly in the real estate industry. The nature of advertising in this business further exposes professionals and makes it easier for potential clients or strangers to contact them. Your face becomes your business card, visible both online and in print through social media, websites, and other mediums.

When I entered the residential real estate field at the age of forty, my face and cell phone number were prominently displayed on signs to facilitate communication with potential buyers. This opened the door to unwelcome late-night calls or invitations to questionable parties. I once received text messages from a man who claimed to be a former deejay. He emphasized his perception of my attractiveness and speculated about my personality before suggesting I leave real estate to pursue modeling. It became evident that he had obtained my contact information from an open house advertisement I published that week. Recognizing the potential danger, I reached out to a friend who was a police officer and, luckily, he was available to serve as my safety contact in case the messenger appeared at the property. Fortunately, he did not.

You might find yourself reflecting on similar experiences. Unfortunately, acknowledging the unwelcome attention that comes with being a woman is a reality that we must accept and navigate as best we can. Establishing clear boundaries and communication strategies can help ensure our safety. Maintain unwavering boundaries, both in actions and dialogue.

During the formative years of my business, I was in a committed relationship with my therapist who advised me never to mix business with pleasure. I adopted his advice and learned to confidently state, "I don't mix business with pleasure." This mantra allowed me to build my reputation while preserving personal boundaries. I developed safety protocols and plans to protect myself when showing properties to strangers.

Building my business from scratch has been a personal accomplishment that fills me with pride. Despite encountering men who sought to undermine me or diminish my achievements, I persisted. Do not wait until the age of 50 to realize your self-worth. You are worth more than someone attempting to steal your light and claim a piece of you. You are deserving of respect and worth so much more than the negative influences that may cross your path.

Throughout my journey, I have learned to stand strong, assert my boundaries, and prioritize my safety. By sharing my experiences and insights, I hope to empower others, particularly women, to navigate the challenges of the industry while maintaining their well-being and self-worth. You have the strength to create a business and a life that honors and uplifts you and is free from the shadows cast by those who seek to diminish your light.

As you find success in the industry, consider the potential impact on your personal relationships. If you have already delved deep into understanding your own identity and the values of your firm, this process may have prompted you to reflect on other aspects of your life, including your personal relationships. Be aware that your personal success, both in terms of financial gain and personal growth, can influence your personal life.

As you achieve success in the industry, carefully consider the potential impact on your personal relationships. Building a thriving business and experiencing personal growth can often lead to significant changes in various aspects of your life. Be aware that your personal and financial achievements can have profound effects on your personal life, including your relationships with loved ones.

One of the primary factors that can affect your success in real estate is the amount of time and commitment required for your business. Particularly during busy periods, you may find yourself spending more time away from home or being unavailable for family events, date nights, or other social engagements. These time commitments can potentially strain your personal relationships, as they may require adjustments and sacrifices from both you and your partner.

Recognize the potential challenges that arise when balancing a thriving real estate business with a fulfilling personal life. Some strategies and approaches can help you navigate these challenges and establish a healthy equilibrium.

First and foremost, engage in open and honest communication with your partner. Initiate a heartfelt conversation about what success means to you, your partner, and your relationship as a whole. By understanding each other's perspectives, desires, and expectations, you create a shared vision for the future that aligns with both of your goals. This open dialogue serves as a foundation for mutual support, understanding, and collaboration.

When discussing the potential effects your success could have on your personal life, emphasize the importance of maintaining a healthy work-life balance. Express your commitment to your partner and family to reassure them that, despite the demands of your business, you value and prioritize your relationships. Together, explore ways to navigate the challenges, distribute responsibilities, and find creative solutions that works for everyone.

Creating a business in real estate often necessitates sacrifices from both partners. It may involve giving up personal time that you previously had, reassessing and redistributing household duties, or coordinating co-parenting schedules, if applicable. Approach these challenges as a team and support each other as you find ways to share the load. By openly communicating about your respective needs and expectations, you establish a supportive and collaborative environment that fosters growth, both personally and professionally.

One effective technique for balancing personal and professional commitments is implementing time blocking. Time blocking involves allocating specific time slots for different activities to ensure that you dedicate quality time to your partner and family. By incorporating intentional time blocks for family events, date nights, and other important occasions, you demonstrate your commitment to maintaining a healthy personal life. This technique also allows you to prioritize and organize your work responsibilities more efficiently to reduce the likelihood of feeling overwhelmed or neglecting your personal relationships.

Regularly reassess and adjust your priorities as your real estate business evolves. Keep an open mind and be willing to adapt your schedule and commitments as necessary. Flexibility accommodates the needs of both your business and your personal life. Continuously evaluating and refining your time management strategies enables you to strike an appropriate balance that sustains your professional success while nurturing the well-being of your personal relationships.

In addition to time management, nurturing a supportive network can also contribute to maintaining a healthy work-life balance. Surround yourself with people who understand the demands of your profession and value the importance of personal connections. This network can provide emotional support, offer advice, and share experiences that enable you to navigate the challenges with greater ease.

Achieving success in real estate does not mean sacrificing your personal life entirely. Prioritize your relationships and make intentional efforts to nurture them. Take the time to engage in activities that foster connection and create lasting memories with your partner and loved ones. Whenever possible, incorporate family members into your business to help them feel included.

Working with buyers and sellers can be an incredibly stressful process. The stakes are high, and your clients are making some of the most significant financial decisions of their lives. As their agent, a significant portion of your time is spent keeping their nerves in check, providing reassurance, and remaining stoic despite any personal challenges you may be facing.

Your clients' investments and transactions become your top priority, and that requires you to put your own feelings on the back seat. The pressure to deliver the best outcomes for your clients often takes a mental or emotional toll on you, but this is something that you must come to terms with as part of your role.

Throughout the buying or selling process, clients may experience anxiety, uncertainty, and even moments of panic. Your ability to remain calm, composed, and reassuring is what guides them through the journey. You become their source of stability and expertise, and help them navigate the complexities of real estate transactions.

While you prioritize your clients' needs, acknowledge and address the impact this can have on your own well-being. The constant management of emotions, the weight of responsibility, and the stress of meeting deadlines and expectations can accumulate over time. To cope with the mental or emotional toll, develop effective self-care strategies. Recognize the importance of maintaining your mental and emotional health, as it directly affects your ability to provide quality service to your clients. Take breaks, set boundaries, and engage in activities that help you recharge and reduce stress. Whether it's spending time with loved ones, pursuing hobbies, or seeking support from a network of peers and professionals, find outlets for self-care.

Fostering open communication and a strong support system can help alleviate the burdens you may face. Connect with colleagues, mentors, or industry associations to share experiences, seek advice, and gain perspectives from others who understand the unique challenges of the profession.

While it is vital to prioritize your clients, it is equally important to prioritize yourself. Acknowledge your own feelings and emotions, and seek ways to manage them. By finding a balance between supporting your clients and taking care of your own well-being, you can navigate the stressors of the industry with resilience and maintain a fulfilling career.

The question of whether it is possible to pursue new love or foster a new relationship while building a business is a complex one. Drawing from personal experience, I would initially lean toward saying no. In retrospect, I realize that during my own journey, my priority was focused on establishing security and stability, which often meant sacrificing personal time for romantic pursuits.

In the process of working with buyers and sellers, the levels of stress are usually extremely high. Despite what you may be managing yourself personally, a lot of your time with clients is spent keeping their nerves in check, remaining stoic, and reassuring them during transactions. Your client's priority is investing in what is generally their biggest financial decision.

The years spent dedicated to building my business, with a primary focus on financial security, laid the foundation for unsuccessful relationships with potential partners. Additionally, the demands of my business affected the time I spent with my family. While I cannot completely express regret for the rapid growth I pursued in my career, I acknowledge that the time spent away from loved ones is irreplaceable. It is a realization that comes with a tinge of sorrow as I recognize that the balance between my work and personal life was tilted heavily toward the former.

I am blessed to have incredible children who understood the challenges we all faced as a result of the sacrifices I made in pursuit of my professional goals. While our family benefited from taking vacations and enjoying certain comforts, there were moments where I realized that I was not clear on my why. This lack of clarity had a direct impact on the time I dedicated to personal relationships and the missed opportunities for quality moments.

Business should not come at all costs, whether it is at the expense of safety or personal time. The purpose of a business is to serve as a vehicle for expanding your life and the lives of those closest to you—perhaps those individuals you identified within the confines of your one-inch-by-one-inch paper; however, when the cost of pursuing business success becomes too high, the monetary gains cannot compensate for the losses incurred in other aspects of life.

Finding a balance between business and personal relationships is a delicate endeavor. It requires thoughtful reflection, open communication, and a deep understanding of personal values and priorities. While it may not be easy, it is possible to establish a healthy equilibrium. It begins with a conscious effort to prioritize personal connections, set aside dedicated time for nurturing relationships, and be fully present during those moments.

Recognizing the importance of spending quality time with loved ones and making intentional choices to prioritize personal connections can help foster new love or strengthen existing relationships. It may involve adjusting work schedules, delegating responsibilities, or seeking support from trusted individuals to create space for personal growth and meaningful connections.

In the pursuit of success, remain mindful of the broader purpose behind your endeavors. True fulfillment comes from finding harmony between professional achievements and personal relationships. It requires finding a rhythm that allows for personal growth, shared experiences, and a deep sense of connection with those who matter most.

While it may initially seem challenging to pursue new love or nurture relationships while building a business, sacrifices made solely for professional gains can have long-lasting consequences. By consciously prioritizing personal connections and valuing the importance of quality time, it is possible to strike a balance between business endeavors and meaningful relationships, which lead to a more fulfilling and harmonious life.

CHAPTER TWELVE
Sex and Real Estate

*"You are worth more than someone attempting to steal
your light and claim a piece of you."*
—**Marcia Bergen**

CHAPTER SUMMARY

Drawing from personal experiences, in this chapter I unveiled the safety challenges and compromises women confront in the real estate industry. I highlighted the spectrum of potential dangers, from physical assault to various forms of harassment, which underscore the critical need for safety precautions, personal boundaries, and official protocols. I suggested strategies to implement before and during client meetings such as requesting a photo identification, having a safety contact, and maintaining situational awareness. I also encouraged the use of secondary phone numbers for advertisements and careful social media use. I explored the struggle of balancing a thriving career with personal relationships. I delved into the demanding nature of work-life and its impact on personal relationships by stressing the importance of achieving work-life balance, effective time management, and a supportive network to manage the mental and emotional stress of this high-pressure profession. I concluded with an emphasis on the vital need for women to assert their boundaries, prioritize safety, uphold self-worth, and consciously prioritize personal connections for a fulfilling life beyond work.

REVIEW

While this workbook provides an overview and strategies for safety in real estate, it is not exhaustive. Continue to stay updated on industry safety trends, attend safety training if available, and always maintain situational awareness. Above all, if anything happens that makes you feel unsafe, report it. Your voice could preserve the future safety of yourself and others.

REFLECTION QUESTIONS

1. What are the primary safety concerns highlighted in the chapter?
2. How can the experiences shared in this chapter instigate the development of better practices within the real estate industry?
3. How have your personal relationships been affected by your pursuit of a career in the real estate industry?
4. What actions can you take to protect your mental and emotional well-being while dealing with high-stress situations in the field?
5. Consider the people in your life who are most important to you. Look at the goals you have set for your business– do they include your loved ones?

SCENARIOS

Scenario 1: You're about to meet a potential client at an open house. What steps will you take before arriving at the house to keep yourself safe?

Scenario 2: You are at your best friend's wedding and the ceremony is about to begin when an important client calls and wants to do a final walk-through of their property before having the lawyer prepare the final papers to close the sale. This has to be done right away because the client is flying out of town later that day. You are torn between fulfilling your professional responsibility and maintaining your commitment to your friend. How would you handle this situation?

TO-DO LIST

- Review your current safety protocols and identify areas for improvement.
- Ensure that your online presence is professional and does not compromise your safety.
- Plan and initiate an open and honest conversation with your partner and/or family about your shared vision for the future.
- Implement time-blocking into your schedule to allocate specific time for personal activities—including time to complete the activities in this workbook.
- Write out a list of people who understand the needs of your profession and could form a supportive network.
- Write out a list of self-care strategies to maintain your mental and emotional health.

STEP-BY-STEP INSTRUCTIONS

1. Read the chapter and note the items you would like to incorporate into your business.
2. Complete the reflection questions and scenarios.
3. Work through the to-do list.
4. Review your goals, core values, and vision. Do they align?
5. Review the tools and strategies from previous chapters and continue to synthesize what you are learning into a cohesive plan for your business.

TIPS AND TAKEAWAYS

- Require all potential clients to provide photo identification before meeting.
- Arrange for a safety person to be on call or with you during client meetings, especially in isolated or unfamiliar locations.

- Dress professionally and choose footwear that allows for quick movement.
- Always position yourself closer to an exit than the person you are meeting, and never turn your back on a stranger.
- Limit the personal information you share online and consider using a secondary number for professional communications.
- Trust your instincts. If something doesn't feel right, it probably isn't.
- Regularly update your safety protocols and procedures to adapt to changing scenarios.
- Keep communication channels open with your team. Share experiences and advice on maintaining safety.
- Communicate regularly with your partner to understand each other's perspectives, desires, and expectations.
- Time blocking is an effective technique for managing personal and professional commitments.
- Flexibility is crucial in managing the evolving needs of your business and personal life.
- Surrounding yourself with a supportive network can help you navigate the challenges of your profession.
- Acknowledging and addressing the impact of your work on your well-being to maintain a fulfilling career.

Your own takeaways:

- _____
  _____
- _____
  _____
- _____
  _____

CHAPTER THIRTEEN
Stop and Smell the Roses

*"There is no passion to be found playing small—
in settling for a life that is less than the one
you are capable of living."*
—**Nelson Mandela**

As I write this final chapter, I am compelled to stop and reflect on my own story and the chapters that formed the book entitled *My Life—The Journey of Me.*

Pause and reflect upon your own personal journeys to truly love and appreciate the person you are as well as the person you are becoming. As you've read in previous chapters, when you journey into a business that requires showing up as yourself for others, it can take a toll on your state of mind and cause you to doubt your why, who you are, and the destiny you are building. Life is an ongoing opportunity to reflect on where you have been and where you are going. Throughout life, it is all too common to get tangled in the web of our mistakes and perceived failures. Our own self-criticism can create barriers that hinder us from fully embracing our authentic selves and acknowledging the remarkable progress we have made. It is as if we wear a mask to present a carefully crafted facade to the outside world while, deep down, we grapple with our internal struggles and insecurities.

In the world of real estate, where interactions with people are at the heart of the business, there will be instances where, despite your best intentions and efforts, you may disappoint others. There will be times when you are unable to accomplish the task you set out to achieve, whether it's guiding a buyer in a challenging market or selling a home in a competitive buyer's market. During these moments, reflect on your intentions and approach the situation with grace and humility.

When faced with difficult market conditions, it can be overwhelming and disheartening. Remind yourself that you are only a human operating in a human world. Real estate markets can be unpredictable, as they are influenced by numerous factors beyond your control. While you may have the best intentions and provide honest, data-driven information to your clients, there will be instances where circumstances simply do not align with their expectations. During these times, show yourself grace and practice self-compassion. Recognize that disappointment and setbacks are an inherent part of any business, including real estate. Approach these situations with grace, humility, and a commitment to professionalism so you can navigate the challenges and continue to grow as a real estate professional.

Rather than dwelling on a disappointing experience, use it as an opportunity to reflect on your intentions and approach. Ask yourself if you acted with integrity, honesty, and professionalism throughout the process. If your intentions were pure and your actions were aligned with your core values, you did your best under the circumstances.

Humility is another essential quality to cultivate in the face of disappointment. Understand that you are not infallible and that even the most experienced professionals encounter challenges in their careers. Embrace a mindset of continuous learning and improvement, and recognize that each experience, even a difficult one, contributes to your growth and development.

If you find yourself in a situation where you are unable to meet the expectations of clients, be honest and upfront about the challenges and limitations you are facing. By communicating openly, you build trust and maintain a strong professional relationship, even in the face of disappointment.

Real estate is a dynamic industry, influenced by market fluctuations and external factors beyond anyone's control. While you strive to provide the best possible service to your clients, there will inevitably be times when circumstances do not align with their desired outcomes.

Ultimately, it is through these moments of disappointment that you have an opportunity to demonstrate your character and commitment to your clients. By showing yourself grace and practicing humility, you maintain your integrity, learn from the experience, and continue to provide exceptional service in the ever-evolving world of real estate.

The truth is that we are our own toughest critics. We scrutinize every decision and replay moments of perceived missteps and missed opportunities in our minds. We dwell on what could have been and compare ourselves to others and diminish our own worth in the process. The weight of these self-imposed judgments can be suffocating and can rob us of the joy and fulfillment we deserve. Yet, in the midst of self-doubt, we must recognize that the external world may not fully comprehend the battles we wage within ourselves. Others may see only our achievements, our successes, and the mask we present. They may not be aware of the doubts, fears, and insecurities that plague us in our quiet moments. We must remember that we are not alone in this struggle. It is a universal human experience to wrestle with our own imperfections and seek acceptance and validation.

Recognizing the importance of our intentions rather our mistakes is what sets us apart as individuals and defines the life we are destined to live. It does not matter where things go wrong if your intentions are pure and your intentions come from your deep-rooted sense of self and values.

To truly embrace who we are and appreciate the journey we have undertaken, we must learn to practice self-compassion. We must acknowledge that we are deserving of love, understanding, and forgiveness, just as we would extend those sentiments to a cherished friend. By cultivating self-

compassion, we can release the grip of self-criticism and create space for personal growth, acceptance, and self-discovery.

While meditation may not be for everyone, there are various ways to incorporate moments of mindfulness into everyday life. Engaging in activities that bring joy, such as walking
in nature, practicing yoga, or engaging in creative pursuits,
can serve as forms of meditation in their own right. The key is
to find practices that resonate with our individual preferences
and allow us to connect with our inner selves.

I personally do not engage in lengthy meditation sessions.
Instead, I practice manifestation and gratitude during solitary
moments throughout my day to remind myself of how far I
have come. I have put my faith in the belief that carving out
the entire path to my destination is not solely my responsibility, but rather a calling from the universe. My sole purpose is
to show up, listen, and be receptive.

As we navigate our personal journeys, we recognize the
role of faith and the greater universe. While we may feel that
the path to our desired destination is solely in our hands,
there are still forces that are beyond our control. There are
moments when we must surrender to the guidance of the universe and trust that it will lead us to where we are meant to
be. This surrender is not a sign of weakness but rather an act
of courage and trust.

By relinquishing the need for complete control, we open
ourselves up to the possibilities and opportunities that lie
ahead. We create space for serendipity and synchronicity to
work their magic and guide us toward experiences and connections that align with our highest good. It is through this
surrender that we find a sense of peace and fulfillment, and
know that we are not alone on this journey.

One powerful way to shift our perspective is to reframe
our perception of mistakes and failures. Instead of viewing
them as signs of inadequacy or unworthiness, we can choose
to see them as valuable opportunities for growth and learning.
Each misstep, each detour, and each setback provides lessons

and insights that shape us into the resilient individuals we are today.

Gratitude allows us to shift our focus from what is lacking to what is abundant in our lives. It opens our hearts to the beauty and blessings that surround us each day. When we practice gratitude, we acknowledge the contributions of others, the support we receive, and the experiences that shape us. It is through gratitude that we begin to realize the depth of our own resilience, strength, and capacity for growth.

Success is not defined by the absence of mistakes but rather by the courage to continue forging ahead despite them. The path to success is rarely a straight line. It is filled with twists and turns, and peaks and valleys. The bumps along the way serve as reminders of our resilience and determination. They test our resolve and provide us with the strength to overcome obstacles and reach new heights. As Miley Cyrus beautifully sings in her song "The Climb," it is the journey that matters most. It is in the moments of uncertainty, the times we face our fears, and the instances where we must summon our inner strength, that we truly discover who we are and what we are capable of achieving.

In the pursuit of our dreams, we must learn to find solace in the small victories and celebrate our progress. Life is not solely about achieving grand milestones; it is about cherishing the moments that make up the fabric of our existence. By cultivating an appreciation for the present moment and finding joy in the simple pleasures of life, we can cultivate a profound sense of gratitude.

My personal recognition comes from the understanding that the modest paper bag ribbons that once adorned my Christmas tree are what evoke identical feelings and memories such as a lavish journey to Europe where I invited my entire family owing to my financial success. Authentic beauty is unearthed in the unremarkable moments we often disregard when we achieve success and embrace a changed way of life. Acknowledging the importance of our previous encounters and the memories formed in diverse situations is where the true gratification of our achievements is attained.

Throughout this journey, foster self-awareness and mindfulness. Taking the time to connect with ourselves on a deeper level allows us to understand our motivations, desires, and values. It enables us to make choices that align with our authentic selves and create a life that is in harmony with our truest aspirations.

In the pursuit of success, keep in mind that it is not solely about achieving external milestones or conforming to societal expectations. True success is a multidimensional concept that encompasses alignment with your values, fulfillment in your relationships, and a sense of purpose and joy in every aspect of your life.

You will come to trust that the path you are on is the right one when the choices you make align with your core values and do not betray your authentic self. Along this journey, you may encounter people who feel insignificant or question their own identity when you establish boundaries that reflect your values. It is through the growth of your business and the evolution of your life beyond imagination that you inspire and empower both yourself and those around you.

To again quote Brené Brown, "You are the wilderness." There will be instances during your pursuit of success when you are called to walk alone. It may feel intimidating, and at times you may question whether you can continue, but you possess the strength and resilience to persist.

Embrace the solitude and find solace in knowing that you are forging your own unique path. It is in these moments of solitude that you discover your true capabilities, develop unwavering self-belief, and tap into a wellspring of courage. Embrace fear and uncertainty, for they are the catalysts that propel you toward growth and transformation.

I encourage you to reflect on your personal journey. Release the grip of self-criticism and acknowledge how far you have come. Embrace the significance of the small things and find fulfillment in the journey itself. Trust in the calling of the universe and remain receptive to its guidance. Stay true to your values and establish boundaries that reflect them. Walk confidently through moments of solitude, for it is there that you find your inner strength and unleash your true potential. Embrace the unknown and have faith in your ability to overcome challenges. You are the wilderness, and your journey to success is unique to you. Embrace it wholeheartedly, for the rewards that await are beyond measure.

Bob Proctor once wisely said, "How low you have gone is how high you will rise." Stay committed to your path and persevere through challenging times. From my own personal journey, I can truthfully attest that some of my most remarkable moments came during the most difficult times.

As you close this chapter and embark on your next, remember that your journey is unique to you. Embrace it wholeheartedly, trust yourself, believe in your abilities, and continue to write the extraordinary story of your life.

CHAPTER THIRTEEN
Stop and Smell the Roses

"Success is not defined by the absence of mistakes, but rather by the courage to continue forging ahead despite them."
—Marcia Bergen

CHAPTER SUMMARY

In this chapter, I highlighted the roles of reflection, self-compassion, humility, and openness on personal and professional journeys. With an emphasis on the inevitability of setbacks, I reframed them as opportunities for growth and learning to urge you to approach such challenges with grace, honesty, and professionalism. I stressed the importance of positive intentions, personal values, mindfulness, self-awareness, and resilience in pursuing your dreams. I acknowledged the role of the universe and faith in guiding your path and recommended mindfulness practices that resonate with your individual preferences. Because success is not linear, but a winding path, I underscored the importance of finding joy in the present moment and surrendering to the universe's guidance. I concluded by encouraging you to embrace solitude as an opportunity for growth and transformation, and inspired you to embark on your journey toward personal and professional success.

REFLECTION QUESTIONS

1. How do you typically respond to disappointments or setbacks in your work?

2. How can you show yourself more grace and self-compassion during challenging times?

3. Since learning about your why in Chapter 3, has it evolved since completing the activities from Chapter 4 through 13? If so, what has changed?

4. After reflecting on this entire course, what has been your biggest discovery? Do you view yourself and your business differently than you did before turning the first page? Why, or why not?

SCENARIOS

Scenario 1: You are a real estate professional who has just lost a major client due to market fluctuations beyond your control. Despite your best efforts, you aren't able to help your client reach their desired outcome. How would you handle this situation using the principles discussed in this chapter?

Scenario 2: Lately, you've been comparing your success to a colleague who seems to be achieving more. You feel inadequate and full of self-doubt. How can you apply the teachings of this chapter to cope with this situation?

TO-DO LIST

- Write down three mistakes or failures from your past. Beside each one, write about one or more lessons learned from the experience.
- Identify areas where you can show more grace and self-compassion.
- Write down your personal definition of success and how it aligns with your core values.
- Practice a form of mindfulness such as meditation or journaling. Find ways to incorporate those practices into your daily life.
- Review your "Fear Trap" quiz from Chapter 1. Reflect on your original responses. Would you change anything now? If so, what, and how?

STEP-BY-STEP INSTRUCTIONS

1. Read the final chapter and reflect on what you have learned on this journey.
2. Go through the exercises as you look back on what you've learned and how you've grown.
3. Work through your to-do list.
4. Review your goals, core values, business strategies, and mission statement, and reflect on what has changed since you started this journey.
5. Finalize your business plan by completing the final assignment at the end of this workbook Chapter.

TIPS AND TAKEAWAYS

- Embrace your mistakes as opportunities for learning and growth.
- Practice gratitude regularly to cultivate a positive perspective on life.
- Maintain mindfulness and self-awareness on your journey to success.
- Trust in the universe and surrender control when necessary.
- Stay true to your values and authenticity on your path to success.
- Disappointments and setbacks are opportunities for growth.
- Show yourself grace and practice self-compassion.
- Align your professional actions with your core values.
- Cultivate mindfulness through practices that resonate with you.
- Keep a daily gratitude journal.

Your own takeaways:

- _____
  _____
- _____
  _____
- _____
  _____

FINAL ASSIGNMENT
Creating Your Business Plan

*"Success is not defined by the absence
of mistakes, but rather by the courage to
continue forging ahead despite them."*
—Marcia Bergen

FINAL EXERCISE—THE BUSINESS PLAN

We've discussed and reflected upon several components across our journey that can now be assembled into your business plan. This exciting process enables you to combine your mission, research, strategy, and goals into a document that showcases your ability to visualize and plan your business's execution.

Now is the time to consolidate, write, review, revamp, and refine your business plan to integrate everything you've learned and reflected upon.

Follow this 10-step guide as you work through the process:

Define Your Core Values, Vision, and Mission Statement: Refer to Chapter 3 and review your core values and mission statement. Finalize a compelling mission statement that encapsulates your purpose and aligns with your core values.

Define Your Goals: Clearly define your short-term and long-term goals to ensure they are SMART: specific, measurable, attainable, realistic, and timely. Detail the actions that will help you achieve these goals.

Describe Who You Are and What You Bring to the Table: In Chapter 5 you read about establishing a strong personal brand that sets you apart from other real estate agents. Align your brand with your personality type, as covered in Chapter 3, and describe what makes you a potent real estate entrepreneur while encapsulating your real estate persona.

Define Your Value Proposition: Chapter 8 defined and explored your value proposition. Clearly articulate what makes your services unique, why clients should choose you over others, and how you intend to deliver this value.

Define Your Buyer Persona: Articulate your buyer persona or target market (Chapter 4). Demonstrate your comprehensive research and show that you understand who your clients are and what their needs entail.

Analyze Your Target Market: Your market research, as discussed in Chapter 4, demonstrates your understanding of the local industry, competitors, and potential customer segments. Highlight your considerations of factors like age, gender, location, interests, income level, and lifestyle, as well as general trends and opportunities in your chosen market.

Outline Your Marketing and Communication Strategy: Explain your comprehensive plan for promoting your services, which should include a branded marketing strategy, a communication plan, and a social media strategy.

Prepare Your Financial Plan: Outline all the anticipated costs (Chapter 2) associated with starting and running your real estate business. Include your revenue model and demonstrate that you have a solid understanding of your finances, operating and marketing costs, budget, and financial goals.

Outline Your Strategy for Long-Term Operation and Growth: Identify key performance indicators that will measure your success. Outline your plans for potential challenges and growth opportunities. Identify your strengths, weaknesses, opportunities, and threats.

Review, Monitor, and Evaluate: Regularly review your business plan. Analyze and monitor your metrics and finances. Ensure that your marketing and growth strategies are hitting their targets and that you're achieving your goals. Continually evaluate, adjust, and revisit.

By following this guide, you'll create a comprehensive and well-rounded business plan that will set you up for long-term success as a business owner in the real estate industry.